COLOURWASH QUILTS

A PERSONAL APPROACH
TO DESIGN & TECHNIQUE

Deirdre Amsden

Colourwash Cross III
by Deirdre Amsden, 1990, London,
England, 24¹/₂" x 24¹/₂".
Collection of Pamela J. McDowall.

Title Page Photo:
Colourwash Overlay II by Deirdre
Amsden, 1986, Cambridge, England,
25" x 25". This small hanging is closely
stipple quilted all over. Collection of
Hawke's Bay Cultural Trust, New
Zealand. Photograph by the author.

Credits

Editor-in-Chief . . . . Barbara Weiland
Technical Editors . . . . Sharon Rose
                                      Barbara Weiland
Managing Editor . . . . Greg Sharp
Copy Editor . . . . Liz McGehee
Proofreader . . . . Tina Cook
Text and Cover Design . . . . Joanne Lauterjung
Production Coordinator . . . . Sandra Seligmiller
Photography . . . . Brent Kane
Illustration . . . . Deirdre Amsden

Colourwash Quilts: A Personal Approach to Design & Technique©
© 1994 by Deirdre Amsden
That Patchwork Place, Inc.,
PO Box 118, Bothell, WA
98041-0118 USA

Printed in Hong Kong
99 98 97 96 95 94   6 5 4 3 2 1

MISSION STATEMENT

WE ARE DEDICATED TO PROVIDING
QUALITY PRODUCTS THAT
ENCOURAGE CREATIVITY AND
PROMOTE SELF-ESTEEM IN OUR
CUSTOMERS AND OUR EMPLOYEES.

WE STRIVE TO MAKE A DIFFERENCE
IN THE LIVES WE TOUCH.

That Patchwork Place is an employee-owned,
financially secure company.

Library of Congress Cataloging-in Publication Data
Amsden, Deirdre,
    Colourwash quilts : a personal approach to design and technique / Deirdre Amsden.
      p. cm.
    ISBN 1-56477-051-6 :
    1. Patchwork—Patterns. 2. Color in textile crafts. 3. Quilting—Patterns. I. Title.
TT835 .A49 1994
746.46—dc20
                                      94-6368
                                           CIP

Dedication

*To my parents, Jean and Ronald Amsden,
with love.*

Acknowledgments

For help with this book, I would like to thank:

The staff of That Patchwork Place, who have guided me through unknown territory with patience, professionalism, and kindness;

Nicky Herbert, who taught me to use a word processor and answered all my anguished cries for help with calmness and good humor;

My parents, who read drafts, made helpful suggestions, and encouraged me throughout, as did the rest of my family;

Jean Amsden, Pauline Austin, Janice Blackhurst, Carolyn Ferguson, Katharine James, Anne Moffat, Kandy Newton, Joanna Richardson, Diana Ridsdill-Smith, and Nancy Sharpe, members of The Cambridge Quilters of England, who took up the challenge of making Colourwash cushions with enthusiasm;

Members of the Marsh Quilters of England, led by Janice Gunner, who made the "Sweet Pea Pinwheel" quilt, and Ann Piper, who lent the quilt for artwork;

Jean Amsden, Barbara Close, Pam Dempster, Jean Draper and Ken Jones, Jenny Hutchison, Gabrielle King, Pamela J. McDowall, Polly Mitchell, and Dieuwke Philpott, who generously lent quilts from their collections for photography; and to those who granted permission for photographs of quilts they own to be published in this book.

The Scandinavian Embassy in London and the Color Institute in Stockholm for information about the Natural Color System.

And finally, I acknowledge the inspiration and friendship of many quilters.

Colourwash Cross IV
*by Deirdre Amsden, 1992, London, England, 24½" x 24½".
Collection of Barbara Close.*

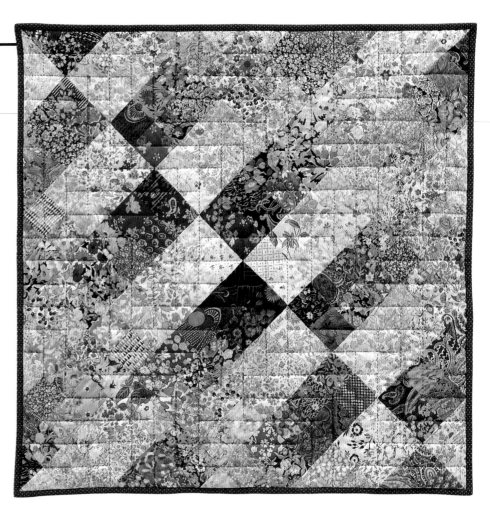

Colourwash Stripe II *by Deirdre Amsden,*
1986, Cambridge, England, 22" x 22".
Collection of Dieuwke Philpott.

CONTENTS

Preface   6

How to Use This Book   7

Introduction:
The Story of Colourwash   9

PART ONE: *Design and Planning   17*

PREFACE

Colourwash Diamond *by Deirdre Amsden, 1992, London, England, 25" x 25". Collection of Gabrielle King.*

Prompted by enthusiastic students and workshop organizers, I had already considered writing about my Colourwash techniques when Nancy J. Martin, president of That Patchwork Place, suggested I write this book. I had put the idea on hold because I did not think such a specialized subject would interest a British publisher. I also imagined that my quilts, being so English in style, would not have a wide appeal. The former situation has probably not changed significantly, but the latter has. With the increase in popularity of international quilt conferences and exhibitions, quilters the world over are now interested in and curious about each other's work. These conferences also provide a meeting place for quilters from many countries to exchange ideas. I first met Nancy at Symposium '89, held in Hastings, New Zealand. I like to imagine that perhaps a small seed was sown at the time.

I have learnt a lot while writing this book. Trying to explain clearly in words what I do as a matter of course has been a revealing exercise. It is now filtering back into my teaching and quiltmaking, and I hope you find it of interest too.

How to Use This Book

As the subtitle indicates, this book is about my personal approach to quiltmaking: how the idea of blending fabrics together into washes of color, hence *Colourwash Quilts,* materialized; and how, in my tortoise-like way, I have gradually developed this simple idea over the last fifteen years. By the end of the book, I hope you will have gained insight into how I achieve my Colourwash effects, and that you will have found much that is useful for your own work.

I suggest you treat this book as a one-on-one workshop and hope you will question my methods and ideas and think of better ways to do things. In this book, as in my workshops, I am not saying, "This is how it must be done." I am only trying to explain how I have chosen to do it. You may choose to do it that way, too, or perhaps you will think of a better way.

The book has four main sections: Design and Planning, Technique and Construction, application in the form of Projects, and General Instructions. This is followed by an appendix that includes grids and useful templates. The Introduction describes how I developed this new quiltmaking technique called "Colourwash." I suggest you scan the whole book quickly to gain an overall understanding, then read it more carefully with a view to practicalities. Once you are familiar with it, you will be able to dip in and out as you please. Page references throughout the text should facilitate this.

The first section contains a series of exercises that I hope you will find helpful and fun to do. The second section details how to go from design to fabric. Seven projects with full instructions are included in the third section of the book.

Although I provide some general sewing and quiltmaking instructions, beginning on page 107, the book focuses on techniques that are unique to Colourwash. If you are a newcomer to quiltmaking, you will almost certainly need other books (or a class, or a friend) to help you learn the basics. I have included several excellent ones in the book list on pages 144–45.

Quiltmaking is a tactile medium and demands hands-on experience. A book can be an excellent guide, but eventually you need to make your own discoveries. Try not to be fearful of making mistakes. After all, mistakes force you to find solutions, which is the way human beings learn. If you play it safe to avoid making mistakes, you miss opportunities that can lead you to new ideas or to questions you might not otherwise have asked. A mistake can also reinforce your original idea, allowing you to resume work with confidence. Instead of throwing unfinished work into the proverbial cupboard every time you meet a problem, use your seam ripper and try again. Even if you are unable to solve it completely, the next time you reach the same point, you will be able to deal with it more successfully and move on. The sense of achievement more than compensates for the struggle.

I cannot think of any quiltmaking rules; however, I try to go by this simple code:

Don't be afraid to make mistakes.

Keep an open mind.

Take time to think and question what you are doing.

Be true to yourself.

Above all else, enjoy making quilts.

INTRODUCTION
THE STORY OF COLOURWASH

Colourwash Overlay III *by Deirdre Amsden, 1992, London, England, 21½" x 21½".*
Collection of Jean Draper and Ken Jones.

"Colourwash" is the term I use to describe laying down a graded wash of color, using small patches of fabric. Like any new idea, the technique is the result of years of experimentation and countless influences. This introduction is an attempt to connect all the seemingly unconnected events that led me to create Colourwash quilts.

Quiltmaking was not handed down from generation to generation in my family. My mother is a self-taught quiltmaker, as am I. My grandmother was a teacher and campaigner who encouraged her children to set their sights on a university education. My mother is artistic and probably would have enjoyed art school, which my grandmother regarded as a frivolous waste of intelligence. I think it is no accident that my brother and sister and I all attended art school.

By the time my mother began quiltmaking in the 1950s, patchwork and quilting had virtually become separate crafts in Britain. Among the numerous Grandmother's Flower Garden and Star designs my mother made, I particularly remember her wreath and garland designs. They were inspired by a quilt from Averil Colby's book *Patchwork*. (See the book list on pages 144–45.) The central wreath and outer garlands were made from assorted floral prints, with larger prints in the middle gradually giving way to smaller flowers and wispy foliage at the edges.

My mother insists I learnt to sew at school, though sewing was an everyday activity in our home. Indeed, I remember with pleasure primary-school needlework lessons held under the trees in summer and around the stove in winter, always accompanied by stories. Pleasant as these early memories are, I owe my real expertise to a strict teacher at secondary school who taught needlework with the seriousness of an academic subject. She did not even allow us to use a sewing machine until we had completed a hand-sewn garment with set-in sleeves, yoke, collar, cuffs, pockets, and buttonholes. I cannot imagine this regime suiting today's students— indeed, it did not suit some of my fellow pupils, but I enjoyed it and am tremendously grateful to her.

I did not continue this training by studying textiles at art school. If I had, it is possible my approach to

Circular Patchwork Tablecloth *(detail) by Jean Amsden, 1985, Linton, Cambridgeshire, England, 66" across. This is one of my mother's favorite designs. She first discovered it in 1960 in Averil Colby's book* Patchwork *and has since used it for several quilts and hangings.*

textiles might have been quite different. Instead, I trained as an illustrator and went on to work as a free-lancer for magazines. My illustrations took the form of photographed collages and three-dimensional models.

I was finally introduced to quiltmaking in a short embroidery course at the Victoria and Albert Museum in London. One afternoon a week, for ten weeks, the instructor demonstrated an embroidery technique and took us into the museum to study examples and gather design ideas. We were then expected to make a sample at home to present the following week.

The course began with patchwork, and I learnt that shapes other than hexagons could be used for patchwork and that shapes could be seamed together by machine! I know this seems inconceivably elementary, but at the time it was a tremendous revelation. An even greater discovery awaited me the second week: quilting. It was like finding the key to a locked door. The possibility of fastening the layers of a patchwork quilt together with simple stitching and glorious texturing was such an exciting realization. I followed the remainder of the course through crewel work, white work, black work, gold work, and so on, all the while researching patchwork and quilting in library books.

It took me three months' practice to learn to quilt with confidence. I even learnt to use a thimble, which neither my mother nor my needlework teacher had been able to coax me to do. I gladly gave up illustration, naively assuming I could earn as much at quiltmaking—but that is another story. In any case, I was well and truly hooked. I often ask myself why it took so long to realize that pattern making is my preferred form of expression and fabric my ideal medium.

The final piece of the puzzle fell into place not long after my conversion to quiltmaking. It was a gift of some Liberty of London™ Tana™ lawn remnants I received from a garment maker who had read about my quiltmaking in the local newspaper. As I was enjoying them in a heap on the floor, I noticed how prettily the colors and prints merged together. So I cut a square from each fabric, blending and shading them

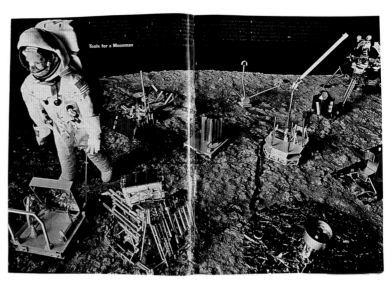

Tools for a Moonman, illustration by Deirdre Amsden, photographed by Julian Cottrell, 1969, London, England. This is typical of my illustration work. It was first published in The Sunday Times Magazine.

THE DECORATIVE ART OF EMBROIDERY

A ten week course

A study of the methods and based on the collection of the Victoria and Albert M

The object of the course its historical context an from which its patterns

The course will be con Mondays from 21 Janu 2 to 4 p.m.

January   21   Patch
January   28   Quilt
February   4   Pull
February 11   Sam
February 18   Ca
February 25   Cr
March   4   B
March 11
March 18
March 25

No previous

Students w
stitches a
an embroi
to work a
threads,

Enrolme
Please
Educat
Victor

V&A
The Decorative Art
of Embroidery

into a crib quilt. To further disguise the patchwork seams, I simply quilted across the squares diagonally. The finished patchwork reminded me of an exercise from art school in which we were required to lay a smooth wash of watercolor paint across a sheet of paper without allowing blotches or tidemarks to spoil the surface. What I had found so difficult to achieve in watercolor was, to my surprise, much easier in cloth. I called the quilt "Colourwash."

Not long after making that first colourwash crib quilt, I came across a fragment of unfinished patchwork I had started in an idle moment while visiting my mother in the early 1970s. She was making a patchwork bikini (seriously!) for a patch-work competition. I remember her trying to persuade me to enter it, too, and sharing her fabrics with me. Not liking the prints, I cut them into small squares and sorted them by value into dark, medium, and light. I then sewed them together in what I now know was a Sunshine and Shadow arrangement. Back at home, away from my mother's example, I neglected to finish the project, and the idea of shading fabric patches by value lay dormant. When I rediscovered the piece, I realized I had thought of blending fabrics together before becoming a quiltmaker and at least five years before making the crib quilt. Even then, it took me another ten years before I fully understood its significance.

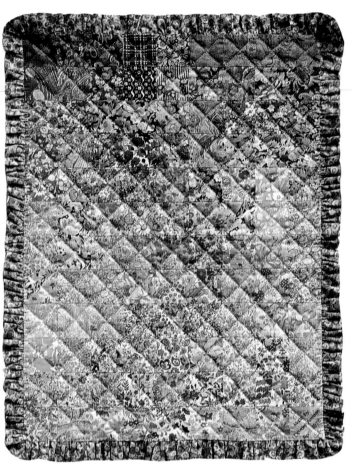

Colourwash Crib Quilt *by Deirdre Amsden, 1978, Cambridge, England, 19½" x 25½", including the ruffle. Machine pieced from 2" squares. Private collection. Photograph by the author.*

Sunshine and Shadow, *detail of an early piece of patchwork by Deirdre Amsden, 1973, Cambridge, England. Hand pieced from 1" squares of lightweight furnishing fabrics.*

The technique I was developing defied the conventional practice of aiming for contrast when creating patchwork patterns, but it was not without precedent. I had always been attracted to scrap quilts—traditional English One-Patch arrangements with their simple shapes. My quilts follow in this tradition, but they differ in one important respect. Whereas the maker of a traditional scrap quilt uses contrast to retain the identity of each patch in the overall design, I do not. I aim to conceal the shapes of the patches, to make an apparently seamless piece of patterned cloth.

Cutting the patches small so the prints do not predominate allows me to use them in this painterly fashion. Aware of the busy surface detail created by myriad colors and prints, I aim to create a simple overall design. On close inspection, the design dissolves and gradually disappears into a spatter of color, only to re-emerge when viewed from afar.

Another great British tradition, Welsh and North Country whole-cloth quilts, suggested that quilting need not be subservient to patchwork, that it need not be restricted to outlining and emphasizing patchwork shapes. These wonderful creations encouraged me to use quilting to disguise patchwork seams and achieve the blended effect I was after.

Chequerboard Quilt, *maker unknown, first half of the nineteenth century, English, 104½" x 107". A great variety of printed cottons, including dress cottons and men's shirtings, were used in this quilt. The maker used a ready-printed center panel, which she surrounded with over two hundred tiny patches and a border print. The quilt is interlined with coarse, hand-woven woolen fabric and quilted through these two layers only. The backing was applied after the quilting was completed. Collection of the Victoria and Albert Museum, London, England. Courtesy of the V & A Picture Library.*

North Country Whole-Cloth Quilt *by Amy Emms MBE, 1982, Bishop Auckland, County Durham, England, 43" x 58". This double-sided quilt features a Cable and Feather border with Scissor and Curled feather motifs and a Square Diamond in-fill pattern, all typical of Emms' quilts. Collection of the author.*

Only with time do we begin to realize which unrelated incidents have influenced our lives and work. Like map references, they help chart a future course. In retrospect, I can point to several nonsewing experiences that gave my quiltmaking its present form.

I remember seeing hidden shapes and faces in curtain and wallpaper patterns in the rooms of my childhood. Once seen, they would remain lurking, and the real pattern could never re-establish itself completely. I still cannot live comfortably with patterns without analyzing them to bits. By cutting prints into small pieces, the repeats and hidden patterns vanish. This probably accounts for my preference for swatch books and dressmaking scraps rather than bolts of fabric. Nor is my obsession restricted to fabric. As a child, I spent hours excavating fragments of broken china from the garden, and in Barcelona I was fascinated by the architecture of Antonio Gaudi and his decorative use of broken tiles and ceramics.

I also vividly remember being taken to see Monet's *Water Lilies* in the Galleries de l'Orangerie on a wet Paris afternoon when I was about thirteen. My family and I were alone in the two oval galleries surrounded by vast paintings of water, willows, and lilies—nothing defined, everything suggested.

In common, it seems, with most of the British race, I love gardens (but not gardening). I am sure this love has seeped into my work as well. I am particularly fond of the gardens of Anglesey Abbey, a few miles outside Cambridge. Here each garden reaches perfection at a different time of year. My favorite is the semi-circular Herbaceous Garden surrounded by tall, dark green beech hedges, which make a perfect backdrop for the magnificent traditional borders.

Postcards from my collection: Monet's Water Lilies; *Gaudí's Güell Park, Barcelona, Spain; Anglesey Abbey, Cambridgeshire, England.*

In the initial stages of my quiltmaking, I endeavored to produce a variety of designs and, in retrospect, I am glad to have served such an apprenticeship. The first Colourwash pieces were just part of that variety. Quilts in the first series, started in 1978, were all variations of simple shading, and by 1981 I thought I had said all there was to say on this theme. (The crib quilt on page 12 and "Colourwash V" on page 45 are from this series.)

The next series (1984–86) came about in response to a commission from the Bedfordshire County Council Schools Loan Scheme, a collection of art and craft exhibited in the county's schools. I clearly recollect that, as I closed my studio door behind the commissioning officer, the idea of introducing contrast flashed into my mind. Not contrast between patches, but between areas of light and dark. I immediately began sketching striped, quartered, and framed designs. As I worked, I realized I could also create illusions of transparency. ("Colourwash Stripe II" on page 4 and "Colourwash Framed I and II" on page 64 are from this second series.)

These small-scale pieces were all made from Liberty of London Tana lawn. In 1987 it dawned on me that I could use a greater variety of fabrics. After all, I had a large collection of fabrics—why was I confining myself to Tana lawn? This realization, a "Eureka!" for me, coincided with moving into a larger studio. The scale of my work increased immediately, and I discovered that the more varied prints now at my disposal created a far more interesting visual texture. So began my specialization in and full-time exploration of Colourwash. ("Colourwash Stripes" on page 47 was the first of my larger-scale quilts.) The increase in size also allowed me to explore three-dimensional illusions ("Colourwash Cubes I" on page 137) and ideas based on the natural world ("Night-time Blues" on page 107).

In 1991 I took another shuffle forward. It occurred to me that Colourwash could act as a background for brightly colored shapes. This is the idea I am presently developing. In the future, I will continue to draw on the natural world for ideas; the night-sky quilts are only the beginning of these explorations.

What at first appeared to be a limited idea has shown itself to have infinite potential. I find the self-imposed constraints of Colourwash liberating: The more I explore, the more there is to explore. It may seem to the casual onlooker as if I am repeating myself, but each quilt represents a step forward for me. If you compare the crib quilt on page 12 with "Colourwash Stripes and Blue Triangles" on page 96, I think you will see development. Now perhaps you would like to begin your own Colourwash adventure?

PART ONE
DESIGN AND PLANNING

Colourwash Checker-board *by Deirdre Amsden, 1988, London, England, 74" x 74". Shadows falling across a tiled floor inspired this design. The diagonal check is overshadowed by a second, much larger, check. The whipped lines of quilting draw a linear grid in yet another direction. A detail of whipped quilting can be found on page 79.*

PRELIMINARY THOUGHTS

> "Creativity is born of an intimacy between thinking and doing, in the moment when thought and action combine to shape the world around us."
>
> From *The Art of Work* by Roger Coleman

This creative double-act of thought and action—ideas and skill, design and technique—play a role in everything we make. As beginners, we may start by learning basic skills, and as our confidence grows, so do our ideas. This was my approach to quiltmaking. Others though, may be design-led and have to develop their own techniques as needs arise. There are advantages and disadvantages to both approaches. The users of the former may take longer to develop their own ideas but when they do, they are not hindered by lack of skill. Users of the latter may experience frustration until they gain skills, but they are probably more original and free from convention in their designs and ideas.

For skill-led quiltmakers, there is a risk of skill becoming the overriding principle. Technical skill alone is not enough; it is a means of expression, not an end in itself. We may gasp and marvel at the execution of the work, but skill for its own sake is an exercise without soul. A few, though, reach such confidence in their skill that they are able to break free from it, to concentrate on ideas. They seem to recapture a fresh, almost naive, quality in their work without appearing contrived. Most of us fall somewhere in between these two extremes.

Quiltmaking is a visual and tactile medium. Whether we are making a bed covering, wall hanging, or banner; whether we wish to decorate, communicate ideas, or proclaim a message, we need to appeal to the visual and tactile senses. When I first saw quilts hung in a gallery, they were like marvelous paintings, but I knew they offered more than just a visual experience. I wanted to touch and feel them and look at the other side. I would like to have wrapped myself in them.

Why Design?

The human desire to decorate and design is intriguing. Did it start as a desire to beautify or to distinguish? Was it for ritual purposes or for the pleasure of the maker? Did our ancestors decorate and design to impose a sense of order on what they perceived as a chaotic world, or to reflect the structures and patterns of the natural world? My father once showed me some magnified photographs of red spider mites. Each was covered with a unique linear pattern, like our fingerprints. Snowflakes, as we all know, are another example of nature's infinite patterns, as awe-inspiring on a small scale as the universe itself.

Designing is a complex combination of perception, emotion, thought, instinct, influence, and tradition. There are books you can read and courses you can take, but at some point you just have to get down to *doing* it.

Creativity is like climbing an uneven staircase. Sometimes you ascend with ease, but at other times you seem to stay on one level so long that you begin to wonder if there are any more steps. They may seem to go up so steeply you can only surmount each one with a struggle, and sometimes they even go down. However experienced you become, the staircase remains unpredictable, which is the very reason that creative activity is so fascinating, addictive, and exhilarating.

Even though I love making quilts, I sometimes delay the start of a new one. It is as if the time has to be absolutely right. The delay gives me time to think and consider alternatives before I begin. I enjoy this time because, while an idea is in my head, anything is possible and there are no compromises. However, once I start work, I wonder why I put it off.

PRACTICAL AIDS FOR DESIGNING

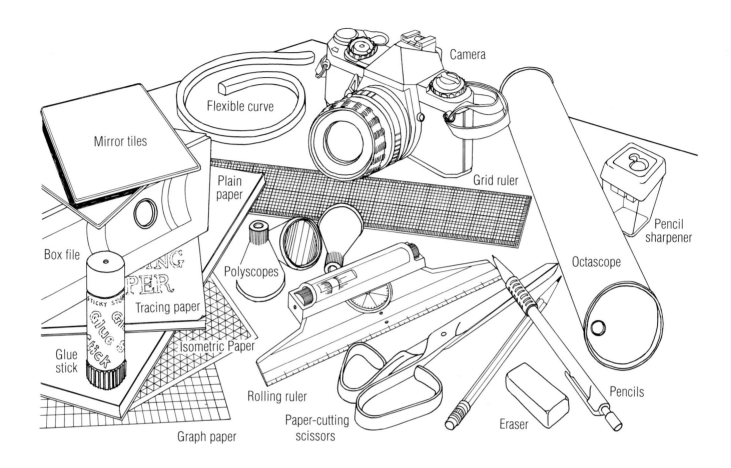

Designing or planning is the first step in the transition from thought to action. A working plan may be anything from sketches and calculations to detailed drawings, full-size cartoons (large-scale preparatory designs), or computer printouts. You can use anything from the humble pencil to the latest technology—anything that suits your working methods and gives you the results you want. Some suggestions:

Drawing, sketching, doodling

Collage: You can cut or tear shapes from paper and glue them into an arrangement, or you can cut apart and rearrange an existing design.

Tracing: This technique enables you to superimpose one image over another, to reverse an image, and to make repeats of a single image.

Photocopying: A photocopier can give you a series of repeats, enlargements, or reductions that you can cut apart and paste into new and different arrangements. (A distortion factor is inherent in photocopiers, so do not use them to copy templates.)

Projection: You can enlarge an image or design to exactly the required size by projecting it onto a sheet of paper taped to a wall and tracing it.

Photography: A camera enables you to easily record design arrangements. A Polaroid camera is particularly helpful because you can see the results immediately. Recording your design arrangements is helpful in decision making or for future reference. Photographs can also be cut up and rearranged.

Light box: This design aid enables you to trace images through ordinary paper or fabric. Before I inherited my present light box from my husband, I made myself one from a drawer, a fluorescent tube, and a translucent sheet of glass. (Do not use an ordinary light bulb as is it emits more heat. A sheet of acrylic is a good substitute for glass.)

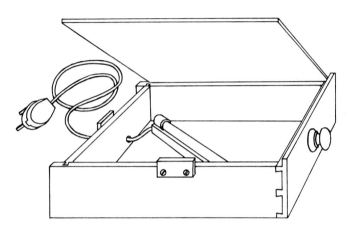

Homemade light box: Pieces of wood screwed to the drawer hold the glass in place.

Mirrors: You can use one of these as a distancing device when arranging patches. (See page 67.) For more information on using mirrors in designing, see pages 22–23.

Window: Cut a shape out of a piece of card stock and use it as a masking or isolating device. Use it to locate and isolate shapes that seem promising as the basis for a design. I used windows during my work as an illustrator to view my models. This gave me an idea of how they would look when photographed. Windows help with color selections (page 54), with purchasing fabric (page 58), and with viewing an arrangement of patches on a flannel wall (page 74). You will find two different types of windows on page 141.

Use a "window" to isolate shapes.

Computer: This marvelous tool is good for repetitive jobs and sorting. Designing involves trying this and that, adding this or subtracting that, which a computer can do with speed (perhaps a little too much speed). Time to think is essential to successful design. Nevertheless, if you have access to a computer, experiment with design programs or take a course in computer graphics to see if it helps you design and plan. Having watched several demonstrations of computer design programs, I can imagine becoming quite addicted to the process—never mind making the quilt.

OBSERVING

> "Artistic perception is often talked about but rarely accounted for. Shrouded in mystery, it is used almost as a justification for the status of art and artists, but to me it is above all, the very simple ability to see freshly, to preserve a momentary experience before the sifting processes of conventional thought cuts us off from contact with the world around us. Far from being a miraculous talent, it is something common to us all, part of a lost childhood, and a skill we need to rediscover."
>
> From *The Art of Work* by Roger Coleman

Every day an enormous amount of visual information bombards us. It's no wonder we learn to block it out, only tuning in when we notice the unexpected. Roger Coleman suggests a way to rediscover the skill of seeing "by playing games that involve looking in categories." Exercises you can do as you walk include picking out shapes and patterns, for example, anything round or spherical or different arrangements of bricks and paving stones. Looking, really noticing, means trying to view the world as if you were seeing it for the first time, like a child or a visitor in a strange country.

Remember what you see by drawing your observations. Drawing is another childhood activity most of us neglect. It forces you to notice details and remember them in a way that photography does not. To conquer your initial reluctance to begin drawing again, I suggest you start by making sketches and jotting down ideas for your eyes only. Do some every day, like a diary, until it becomes a habit. Don't think of these drawings as "art," but as notes to yourself.

At art school I was encouraged to keep a sketch book, but I found it difficult to put everything into one book. My inclination is to sketch and make notes on odd sheets of paper. You can lay loose drawings and clippings out for comparison. You can rearrange them, juxtapose one idea with another, and spot recurring ideas.

Ideas come from the most unexpected places. Train yourself to notice and/or collect objects, sketches, reference books, clippings, photographs, postcards of museum objects—anything that gives you an idea or strikes a cord. These things all provide stepping-stones for developing your own designs. You may have a specific idea and seek out materials to help you execute it, or you may just collect ideas on the off-chance they will come in useful sometime. Use this source material to make an individual and original piece of work.

It is also essential to develop critical awareness. Do this in the privacy of your own home by studying your collection of quilt books. Pick one with a good selection of whole quilts and study each one critically. Analyze what you like or dislike about each one and why. Be constructive and qualify your criticisms. You can do this exercise with a friend—voicing your opinions and arguing your case help to clarify your thoughts. The point of this exercise is to develop objective and constructive critical judgment of your own work.

ELEMENTS OF DESIGN

Shapes (and lines), values, textures, and colors are the basic ingredients or elements from which to choose when designing a quilt. You may decide not to use them all in every quilt. For example, the success or failure of a white whole-cloth quilt rests almost entirely on texture.

Before discussing the elements of design, it is helpful to consider various ways of organizing, or composing, them into a design.

Symmetry and Asymmetry

Symmetrical designs are either bilateral (two halves, one a mirror image of the other) or radial (a repetitive design of any number of sections radiating from a center point).

You can easily create bilateral and radial symmetry by playing with mirrors. Place a mirror diagonally, vertically, or horizontally across an image to make a bilateral design with the same image repeated on each side of the mirror or axis (a design with one plane of symmetry). Hold two mirrors at right angles to produce a radial design in which each quarter reflects the two adjacent quarters, medallion designs for example. Changing the angle of the mirrors changes the number of planes or sections, such as in a mandala design.

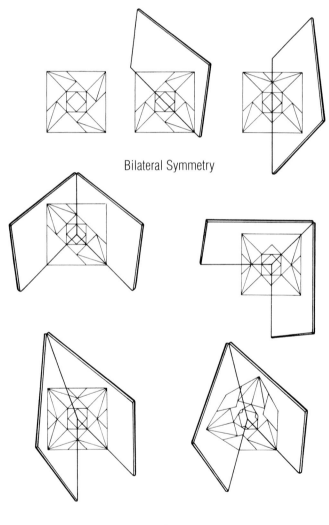

Bilateral Symmetry

Radial Symmetry

Eccentric Star is a block that has neither radial nor bilateral symmetry (no planes of symmetry), but if you place a mirror across it at various angles, you can make several symmetrical arrangements from it.

To assist in designing border patterns, place two mirrors parallel to one another, either at right angles to your design for a straight border, or angled for a zigzag border. Also, moving a single mirror, held at a 45° angle, across a border can help you decide where to turn the corner.

You can place and move your mirror(s) anywhere across a design or block to create new symmetrical designs. Go through this book or any quilt book, playing with mirrors. Discover which quilts are symmetrical in design and alter the asymmetrical ones into various symmetrical compositions.

If you place a mirror diagonally or vertically across the blocks below, you will see they have no planes of symmetry. However, if you rotate the first one through 360°, a symmetry of appearance occurs four times in one full rotation. In the second block it only happens twice, and the third block has to be turned a full 360° before it looks the same again.

Symmetrical arrangements are satisfying and have natural balance.

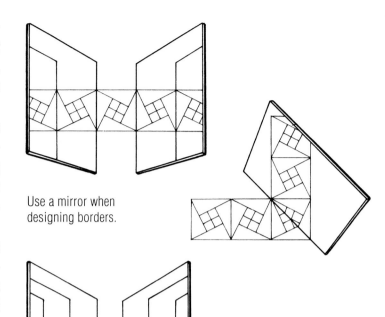

Use a mirror when designing borders.

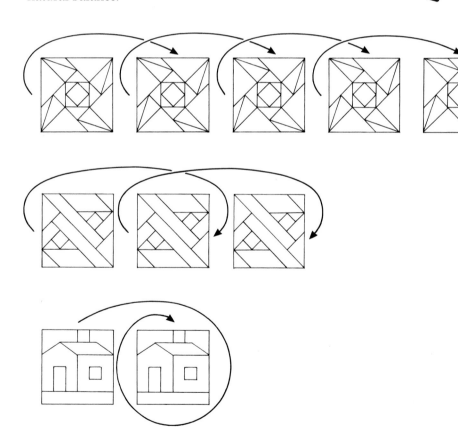

Symmetry of appearance: The top block, Eccentric Star, has a greater symmetry of appearance than the lower House block.

Colourwash Stripes II *by Deirdre Amsden, 1987, London, England, 48½" x 71". This quilt required the same templates as did Colourwash Stripes I on page 47, but the stripes are crosscut at random.*

Though it might appear otherwise, asymmetry is not random. It is planned and balanced but lacks symmetry. There is little symmetry of appearance and there are no planes of symmetry. The eye cannot settle on the expected. It is constantly searching for the repeat and trying to create order.

Asymmetrical arrangements are more dynamic than symmetrical ones. To achieve balance with an asymmetrical arrangement, you have to keep trying it this way and that until it looks right. If it looks right, then it is right. You can also shade or color symmetrical designs asymmetrically to upset their symmetry, or you can distort symmetrical designs into asymmetrical arrangements as shown at right, below.

The Eccentric Star block illustrates three different shading arrangements:

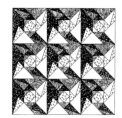

Symmetrical shading, where each part of the block is balanced with its opposite.

Asymmetrical shading within the block is balanced by regular repetition.

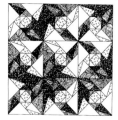

A random arrangement of the asymmetrically shaded blocks. Note that the four blocks in the top right-hand corner just happened to fall together symmetrically.

"The Four Seasons" on page 25 are miniature quilts that may be hung together in symmetrical or asymmetrical arrangements. Some of the different arrangements are illustrated at right. To do this, I attached loops to all four corners and sleeves to all four sides of each quilt.

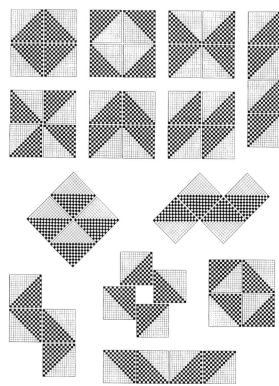

Other possible arrangements for "The Four Seasons"

Random Arrangement: Haphazard, accidental arrangements may not seem a promising starting point for design. Random folds in paper or joining haphazardly scattered dots with straight lines can be the starting point for making patterns. After a while, you will probably find yourself selecting or trying to influence the outcome. Block patterns can also be distorted in a random fashion.

Draw a random grid of lines to correspond in number to your original block. Then, taking a section at a time, transfer the original design onto the distorted grid.

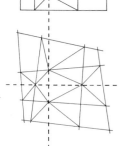

Off-center Distortion

Random Distortion

Repetition: You can introduce symmetry or order into asymmetrical and random arrangements by repeating or mirroring them. I have a couple of polyscopes or faceted lenses, which make repetitive patterns out of random images. It is fun to play with them. One is divided into square facets and is similar to a quilters' multi-image viewer. It makes block repeats. The facets of the other are arranged in strips. It creates strip repeats that move from horizontal, to diagonal, to vertical as you turn the lens. Viewed through these lenses, the world is forever shifting and rearranging. By arranging patterns in sequences, simple repeats, and shifted repeats, or by rotating or reflecting them, you realize there are endless combinations. Add the variables of distortion, superimposing one design over another and changing the shading and colors, and the possibilities are mind boggling.

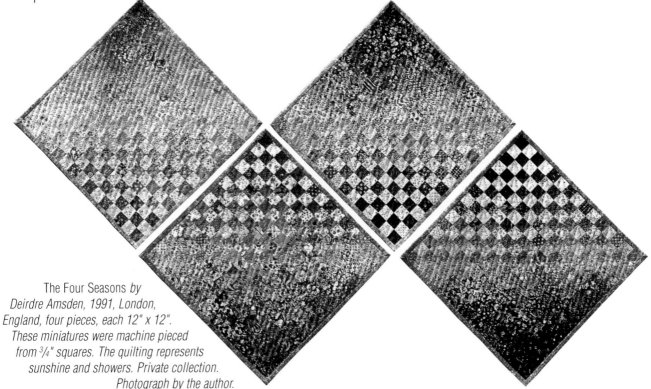

The Four Seasons *by Deirdre Amsden, 1991, London, England, four pieces, each 12" x 12". These miniatures were machine pieced from $^3/_4$" squares. The quilting represents sunshine and showers. Private collection. Photograph by the author.*

Value

Value is the lightness or darkness of colors—the gradation from light to dark. Contrast of values is the degree of difference between values. Value and contrast define patchwork designs. Establishing areas of shading from one value to another and areas of contrast is fundamental to designing for Colourwash. This is my starting point. In my first series of Colourwash quilts, I was concerned with shading only. It wasn't until I introduced contrast in the second series that I was able to develop the idea further. Because value and contrast play such a significant role in my work, I only design in value, that is, black, white, and shades of gray, not in color. (See the design drawings for "Colourwash Stripes I" on page 46.)

Value is relative. A very dark value placed next to a very light one creates a sharp contrast, and the dark appears darker, the light lighter. The strongest, sharpest contrast of all is black and white. A medium value placed next to a medium-dark or medium-light one is less reinforcing and weaker in contrast. (See the scale of contrast below.) Strong contrasts appear to advance. They create areas of high visual tension. Muted or soft contrasts seem to recede and produce weaker tensions. See "Colourwash Stripes I" on page 47 and notice the strong diagonals of sharply contrasting stripes pulling against one another. This effect calms down as the values start to merge.

Two value scales shading in opposite directions give a scale of contrast. At each end of the scale, the contrast between light and dark is sharpest. It diminishes in strength toward the center, where the values are more equal. Sharp, strong contrasts appear to advance, while softer, less defined contrasts appear to recede.

Values exist only in relation to their neighbors. Medium values become light against a dark value but are dark against a light one.

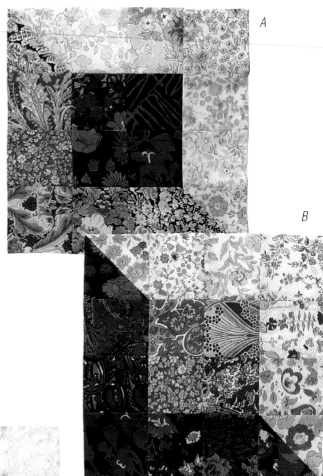

A

B

Relative Values: The dark value in the center of Block A appears stronger in value against the light value than against the medium value. The medium value in the center of Block B appears light against the dark, and dark against the light.

If you wish to use a light color scheme, yet retain value contrasts, discard the darkest values and give the role of dark to the medium-dark fabrics. And of course, you can do the opposite to darken a color scheme.

Colourwash designs can include from two to five values. A greater range becomes confusing unless you limit your use of fabrics, as in the "Crib Quilt for a Summer Baby" on page 87. I don't advise attempting to use five values until you are very comfortable sorting and using four.

Two values: light and dark

Three values: light, medium, and dark

Four values: light, medium-light, medium-dark, and dark

Five values: Very light, medium-light, medium, medium-dark, and very dark

Six or more values: Limit your fabrics to a range that grades from light to dark, but use any number of fabrics you wish. Study the blocks at right to understand values as they relate to each other.

Many of my Colourwash quilts use the relationships between light and dark areas to create a variety of effects that are similar to optical illusions.

Spatiality

Values can create a feeling of space—of some objects or shapes being in front of others, or nearer or heavier than others.

In general, light values appear to advance and dark values to recede. This creates an illusion of depth. However, silhouetting dark shapes against a light background can make the dark values appear to come forward. In "Colourwash Framed IX" on page 28, the "floating frame" shades from light to dark and appears to be in front of a background that shades in the opposite direction. Note that all the values in the floating frame have been made to advance, while in the background they appear to recede.

As a general rule, the eye perceives dark values as heavier than light ones. "Colourwash Framed IX" may appear to be upside down because the background is darker (heavier) at the top, but it is balanced by the floating frame, which is "correctly" weighted by the dark at the bottom.

Two values

Three values

Four values

Five values

Colourwash Framed IX *by Deirdre Amsden, 1990, London, England, 23" x 23". Machine pieced from 1½" squares. Collection of Lynne Edwards. Photograph by Paul Seheult.*

You will observe that many of the quilts in this book are darker at the top, as if the strength of color is draining away. In my night-sky quilts, the light on the horizon is either the dawn of a new day or the last glimmer of the old. I feel comfortable with darks at the top. If it feels unnatural to you, it is probably because the natural order of the landscape, which makes us feel the right way up is: foreground in the darkest values, middle distance in the medium values, and sky in the lightest values.

Dimension

Dimension is similar to spatial illusions, but instead of making objects appear to float in space, dimension creates the illusion that the shape itself has depth. Tumbling Blocks and Attic Windows are familiar examples of three-dimensional illusions created by the positioning of light, medium, and dark values in the design. You create this illusion by imagining a light source and making the planes turned as far away as possible from this "light" dark, as if in shadow. (See "Colourwash Cubes I" on page 137 and "Colourwash Cubes II" and "Colourwash Cubes III" on page 77.) A design can contain several light sources of varying intensity, or the light source can be more intense in one part of the design than in another. It can change direction throughout the design too. Three-dimensional designs can sometimes be hard to "fix" visually. They can suddenly change so that areas you thought were protruding now appear as an indentation. To test this, try looking at Cubes I, II, and III as you turn the book in a complete circle.

Transparency and Shadow

One way to create the illusion of transparency is with color. If, for example, an intermediate shape formed by superimposing part of a blue shape over part of a red one is violet or purple, the colors will appear to be transparent. But illusions of transparency can also be conveyed successfully with strategic placement of value. A dark value superimposed over a light one will appear to be a medium value. (See "Colourwash Overlay II", page 1.)

The easiest way to plan for transparency effects in color or values is to use tissue paper or cellophane. When working with color, choose tissue or cellophane that matches your fabric colors. For value, choose any transparent color or colors. For a design using three values (dark, medium, and light), select a medium-value tissue or cellophane, trace your shapes, cut them out, and paste or lay them in position. Where two shapes overlap, you will perceive a darker value. These areas represent your dark values, the single layer of tissue represents your medium values, and the white background paper your light values.

For designs using four or five values, use two colors of tissue or cellophane.

Transparency using color— blue over red produces an intermediate color, purple.

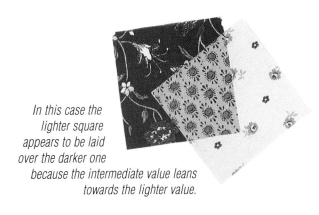

In this case the lighter square appears to be laid over the darker one because the intermediate value leans towards the lighter value.

Here the intermediate value is closer to the dark square; therefore, it seems to be on top of the lighter square.

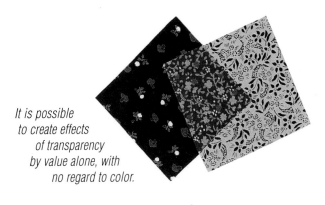

It is possible to create effects of transparency by value alone, with no regard to color.

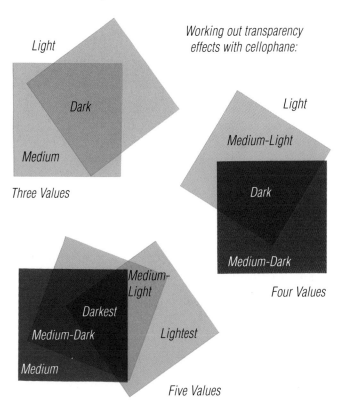

Working out transparency effects with cellophane:

Light
Dark
Medium

Three Values

Light
Medium-Light
Dark
Medium-Dark

Four Values

Medium-Light
Darkest
Medium-Dark
Lightest
Medium

Five Values

"Colourwash Cuboids and Stripes," below, contains both illusions of transparency and three-dimensional illusions.

Effects of shadows are similar to transparency. The areas over which a shadow falls are darker in value. See "Colourwash Checker-board" on page 17.

Colourwash Cuboids and Stripes *by Deirdre Amsden, 1992, London, England, 63½" x 46½". This quilt contains both visual illusions of transparency and three-dimensional illusions. The cuboids and stripes change in intensity from light to dark in opposite directions. The stripes extend beyond the cuboids to form a border.*

Value Exercises

The following exercises are not intended to suggest designs for Colourwash but to help you form the habit of thinking in values when designing. Make several photocopies of the next three pages, and use them to do the following exercises:

Exercise One: Use page 32 to create as many different patterns as possible. Use just three values: solid for dark, lines to represent medium, and blank for light areas. See how many different ways you can shade it, bearing in mind the following suggestions:

    Emphasizing blocks
    Disguising blocks
    Shading alternate blocks differently
    Shading to make linear designs
    Shading blocks symmetrically and asymmetrically
    Random shading

Make several shadings on one photocopy. As soon as you can see a pattern emerging with one shading, start another until the page is used up. Now make several photocopies of your page of shadings, cut each shading apart in any way you like (diagonally, horizontally, vertically, into squares, oblongs, triangles, etc.), and paste the pieces into new arrangements. You can then photocopy your paste-up and cut it apart to make more patterns.

From time to time, play with your mirrors, placing and moving them across the designs you have created to observe further possibilities. (See "Symmetry and Asymmetry" on pages 22–25.)

Exercise Two: Shade in the designs on page 33 to create three-dimensional effects. Imagine a source of light and leave the planes that catch the light blank. Shade those turned farthest away from the light a dark value (solid), and the ones in between a medium value (lines). If you want to introduce more than three values, devise some intermediate shadings, such as dots or cross-hatching, or just use different pressures of solid shading. On a second photocopy, change the direction of your light source or vary its intensity within each design. (See "Dimension" on page 28.)

Exercise Three: Create effects of transparency on page 34, using one tissue paper in a clear color of medium value. Lay the tissue paper over the designs and trace off areas of each design. Cut out the tracings and paste them in position, remembering to overlap them where you require dark values.

Now try the exercise again, using two different colors of tissue paper to create illusions of transparency with four or five values. (See "Transparency and Shadow" on pages 29–30.)

Sometimes it is possible to create three-dimensional illusions or illusions of transparency in designs that are not initially drawn with these in mind.

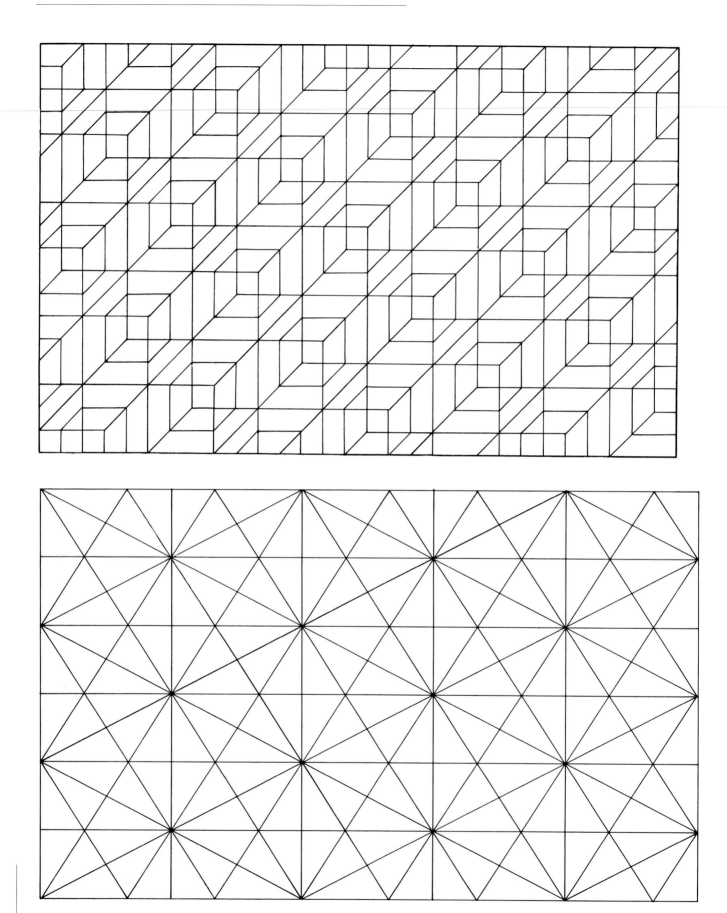

Shapes and Grids

Almost all Colourwash designs are either One Patch arrangements or variations of the One Patch because you need the freedom to move patches from one position to another until the right effect is achieved. Five variations appear in this book:

1. Designs using one basic shape only. The cushions on page 84, for example, were made using only 1½" squares for a total of one template.

2. Designs based on one basic shape and its parts. "Colourwash Stripes I" on page 47 and "Colourwash Stripes II" on page 24 were both made from a 1¾" square and the square cut in half diagonally to form a right-angled triangle, for a total of two templates.

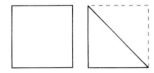

"Colourwash Checker-board" on page 17 required a 1¾" square and two partial squares, a total of three templates.

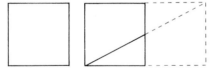

With a total of five templates, "Colourwash Stripes III" is more complex but is still just composed of squares and partial squares. See the design drawing on page 69.

3. Designs using interlocking variations of one basic shape. I made "Night-time Blues" on page 107 by randomly arranging equilateral triangles of three different sizes.

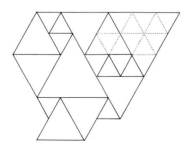

Squares, diamonds, and right-angled triangles of varying sizes also fit together. (See pages 38 and 39.) These interlocking arrangements do not easily break down into blocks or sections and therefore need to be pieced with half seams. (See page 112.)

4. Designs with several basic shapes, where each shape is of a different value. In this arrangement, patches have limited movement confined within their own value. (You can always make up for this lack of flexibility by cutting two different shapes from the same fabric if you think it would be useful.)

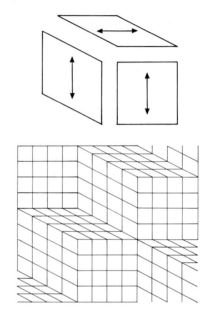

Although "Colourwash Cubes I" (page 137) and "Colourwash Cubes II" and "Colourwash Cubes III" (page 77), do not require different shapes, the diamond template was placed differently according to the value of the fabrics to ensure that the straight grain of the fabric ran in the same direction throughout each quilt.

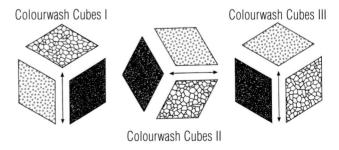

Colourwash Cubes I   Colourwash Cubes III

Colourwash Cubes II

The different placement of dark, medium, and light diamonds on the straight grain of the fabric (indicated by arrows) for Cubes I, II, and III.

5. Designs where part of the basic shape is trimmed off and replaced with a contrasting color. In "Colourwash Stripes and Blue Triangles" on page 96, I positioned the bright colors after I arranged the overall Colourwash. See pages 97–98 for the piecing instructions.

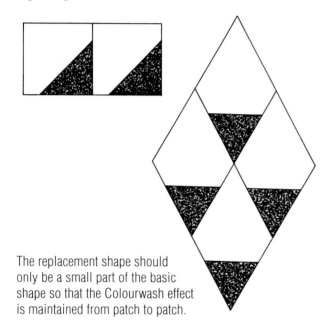

The replacement shape should only be a small part of the basic shape so that the Colourwash effect is maintained from patch to patch.

You can draft most One Patch designs either to scale (for a design drawing) or full size (for templates) on graph or isometric paper. The illustrations on pages 38–39 suggest the variety of shapes you can draw on these two grids. In the Appendix, beginning on page 137, you will also find grids and templates for some of the most useful shapes.

Block Designs

Block designs can be used in a Colourwash arrangement, such as in the group quilt "Sweet Pea Pinwheel" on page 94. Simple counterchange blocks, such as the Pinwheel design, are perhaps the easiest and most suitable. Each block is made from fabrics very close in value, but not identical, so the block design is visible but the block as a whole is either dark, medium, or light. Some simple counterchange blocks are shown on page 40.

It is also possible to adapt some block patterns into One Patch arrangements, and therefore Colourwash shading, and still maintain the outline of the original block. Patterns with a distinctive outline, such as stars, adapt well.

Colourwash Star block by Deirdre Amsden, 1987, Cambridge, England, 9" x 9". This block is a Colourwash version of Ohio Star and was made for a friendship quilt.

1. Draw the block out on graph or isometric paper.
2. Erase all the lines except the outline. Now you can see the basic shapes required to make the Colourwash block (a square and a right-angled triangle) in each of the examples shown on page 37.
3. Make shaded drawings to decide how to shade the block before cutting out the fabric shapes.

Milky Way

Monkey Wrench

Ohio Star

Three traditional blocks—Milky Way, Monkey Wrench, and Ohio Star—are broken down into two simple shapes (square and right-angled triangle) and reconstructed with shaded fabrics.

Simple Counterchange Blocks

Scale

Scale is an important consideration during the planning stage. By scale, I mean the size of your basic shape (square, diamond, hexagon, etc.) in relation to the overall design.

First and foremost, the size and number of your basic shapes determine the size of your quilt. To calculate the finished size, count the number of times your basic shape is repeated horizontally and vertically, then multiply by the size of your basic shape. For example, a design 30 squares wide by 45 squares long made of 1½" x 1½" squares will measure 45" x 67½". If the finished size is too large or too small, you can do one of two things: decrease or increase the number of basic shapes in your design, or change the size of your basic shape. Reducing the basic shape in the example above to a 1¼" square brings the quilt size down to 37½" x 56¼". Enlarging it to a 2" square would make a 60" x 90" quilt.

Record these calculations on your design drawing for future reference and rechecking. At this stage, you can also calculate roughly how many values your design requires and how many pieces you will need to cut from each value, an important consideration when you select fabrics. The number of fabrics at your disposal may determine both the size of your basic shape and the overall size of your project. See the design drawing for "Log Cabin Colourwash" on page 68.

The relationship of scale between the basic shape and the overall size of the quilt is crucial to interpreting your design successfully. I cannot give you any rules: Large quilts do not necessarily require large shapes. The relationship just has to look right. For example, when I was asked to make a smaller version of "Night-time Blues" (page 107), I felt I needed to reduce the scale of the basic shapes, especially the larger of the three triangles. I did not, however, wish to reduce the size of the smallest triangle. Therefore, I had to decide whether to discard the larger triangle and use the remaining two or to use a different basic shape. I chose the latter and used a 1¼" hexagon for "Blues in the Night." See the close-up at right and the complete quilt on page 115.

The scale of fabric prints is another concern, one that is addressed in the chapter on Fabric. (See "Value, Scale, Color, and Texture" on page 59.)

Night-time Blues, *detail showing the three sizes of equilateral triangles. (See page 107 for the whole quilt.)*

Blues in the Night, *detail showing the single hexagon shape. (See page 115 for the whole quilt.) Note how the quilting designs emerge from the busy prints into the areas of plain fabrics and pattern them.*

PLANNING THE BORDERS

Not all quilts need borders but if you intend to add one, try to plan it at the design stage. Borders should not look like ill-considered afterthoughts. It can be sad to see a quilt design imprisoned in an inappropriate border; equally upsetting is a quilt in search of a border. So far, I have had difficulty bordering Colourwash designs with anything but Colourwash borders. To me, an expanse of one print seems at odds with all the fragmented prints, and plain fabrics appear stark and untextured against the busy visual textures of a Colourwash quilt.

Borders serve a variety of functions, including:

- Enclosing a central design, as in medallion designs, which may contain several borders.

- Separating the quilt design from its surroundings like a frame around a painting. Not all paintings are framed and not all quilts need framing. Many of the Colourwash quilts in this book have only the narrowest of borders formed by the binding. I found it difficult to put even that around some of them because I felt the designs could have been continued if I'd had enough fabric, space, or time, for example. The night-sky quilts ("Night-time Blues," page 107 and "Blues in the Night," page 115) were especially hard to limit with a binding because the night sky has no such limit.

- Continuing the central design while at the same time defining a limit. For example, in "Colourwash Cuboids and Stripes" (page 30), the stripes continue and form a border containing the cuboid shapes. This could also be achieved by changing value, making the border either lighter or darker than the central area.

- Providing a floating plane. This is achieved by extending the background into the border. The central design then appears to be floating on its own background.

- Being the main design focus. (See the crib quilts on pages 87 and 91.)

Borders may be single or multiple, wide or narrow. A narrow inner border can be used to separate the main design from a wider border design. If you finish a quilt with a facing or by folding the two edges inward, you free your design from a frame of any kind. Borders do not have to be symmetrical, nor do they have to border every edge of a quilt, but they should relate to and be part of the whole.

Consider all of the options when debating whether or not to add a border. Remain open to change. Once you have made the body of the quilt, you may find that the unbordered design you planned needs a border after all. On the other hand, you might decide to remove a finished border because it does absolutely nothing for the quilt.

TEXTURE

Both tactile and visual texture are used in quiltmaking. There are the textures of different types of fabric; for example, satin and corduroy both feel and look different. Fabrics that feel the same can also have different visual textures. A small dot design appears visually different from a large floral print. (See "Pattern Types" on page 59.)

Patchwork seams also add texture to the surface of a quilt, especially if they are pressed to one side rather than open. Additional texture can be added by folding, pleating, or gathering fabric and by adding embellishments such as beading or embroidery. Quilting is the most obvious texture and the one I use most in my quilts.

Planning the Quilting

Like the border, the quilting should not appear to be an afterthought. Patchwork and quilting are more likely to work together as a whole if they are planned simultaneously. Some traditional British quilts were deliberately double sided—pieced on one side and whole cloth on the other. Mrs. Amy Emms, whose quilt is featured on page 13, often quilts a pieced top from the back, as if she is quilting a whole-cloth quilt. She feels the patchwork interferes with the quilting, which is, after all, her art. People often ask me if I quilt my quilts this way (and it is an option) because they think it must be difficult to mark a quilting design across so many busy print fabrics.

Indeed it is, but the reason I mark the front is because I like to relate the quilting to the patchwork. I use the pieced shapes as a guide for marking the quilting lines even though I am endeavoring to disguise their outline. Occasionally, I use quilting to emphasize certain seams within the pieced design. This requires pressing the seams to one side instead of open. Designing the quilting at the same time as the patchwork allows me to make these decisions in advance, providing some insurance against those inevitable "if only" situations.

While designing the quilting, remember to read about and consider the different quilting effects and options available to you. (See pages 118–26.) The surface of a Colourwash quilt is already so busy that intricate and detailed quilting motifs do not "read." However, this does not mean a Colourwash quilt requires less quilting. *The purpose of quilting a Colourwash quilt is to add texture and to disguise the seaming so the fabrics blend together into a seemingly whole piece of cloth.* If you study the very first Colourwash quilt I made, on page 12, you will see that the simple diamond quilting creates a square-on-point in contrast to the actual patchwork squares.

I find the easiest way to design quilting is to lay sheets of tracing paper over every stage of my design drawings and draw proposed quilting designs in dotted lines, as shown on page 44. This way, the patchwork and quilting evolve together.

Quilting template placement showing the relationship between patchwork shapes and quilting designs in my three night-sky quilts—"Blues in the Night" (page 115), "Day into Night" (not shown in this book), and "Night-time Blues" (page 107) is illustrated below. I often mark out a quilting design with a ruler or a flexible curve, using the pieced shapes as a guide. "Colourwash Checker-board" (page 17) was marked this way.

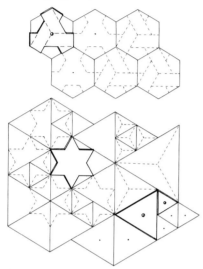

I used a ruler to finish marking *Blues in the Night* after marking around the template. The template fits into the hexagon patchwork shapes. I also used a ruler to mark out *Night-time Blues* once I had marked the center point of each triangle with the aid of templates.

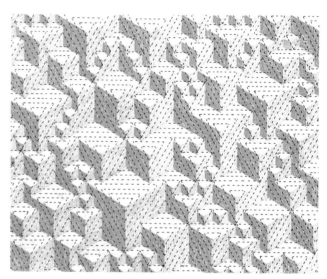

The final quilting designs for Cubes II and III marked out on tracing paper.

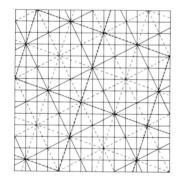

Colourwash Checker-board showing the ruled quilting lines.

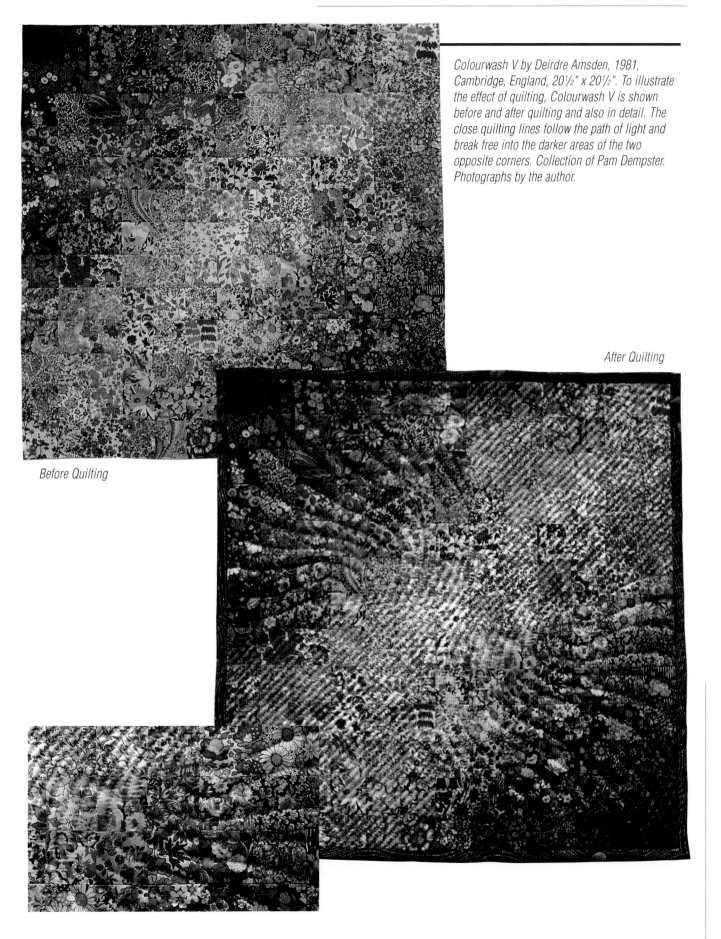

Colourwash V by Deirdre Amsden, 1981, Cambridge, England, 20½" x 20½". To illustrate the effect of quilting, Colourwash V is shown before and after quilting and also in detail. The close quilting lines follow the path of light and break free into the darker areas of the two opposite corners. Collection of Pam Dempster. Photographs by the author.

After Quilting

Before Quilting

WORKING DRAWINGS AND CONSTRUCTION PLANS

My working drawings do not always follow the same formula. I spend a lot of time thinking, doodling, sketching, and making shaded drawings. I use a light box and mirrors and trace, photocopy, cut, and paste. When things start to come together, I begin to think about scale, template shapes, borders, and quilting designs. When I am clear in my mind and my drawing contains enough information, I start working with fabric. I try not to be absolutely specific in the design drawing. If the design spells out every last detail, the rest of the process becomes rote and I lose the chance to explore and discover.

If I am working on a commission and need more than a personal working plan, I make clear drawings and tracings and sometimes even a full-size color mock-up of a section of the design to give an idea of what the finished piece will look like. At other times, I make no drawings at all. The night-sky quilts emerged from a remembered image of a sky full of stars. This memory and photographs of the energy and fury of outer space were my only references.

Although I work from a plan, I keep my options open and remain receptive to new ideas. The working drawing is only a starting point that enables me to move to the next stage. Quiltmaking is a series of stages. Those stages requiring intense concentration are interspersed with repetitive tasks that leave part of your mind free to assess what you have done so far and what you need to do next.

These design sketches for Colourwash Stripes I *reveal how the idea evolved from* Colourwash Stripe III *on page 126. By the third key drawing I had sorted out the zigzag border top and bottom and the overall dimensions which allowed me to start cutting the fabric shapes.*

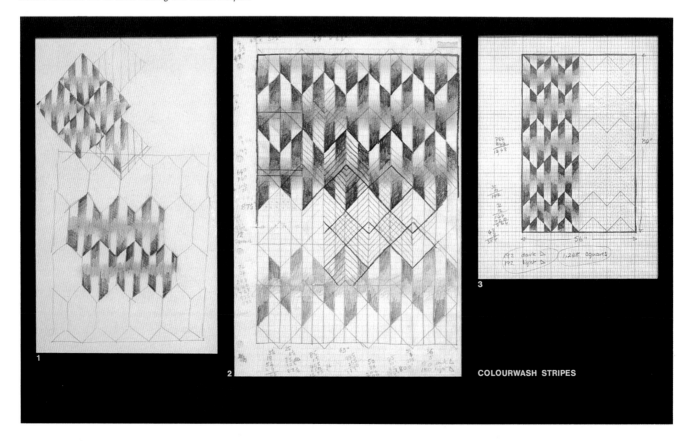

COLOURWASH STRIPES

Use your design drawing to break down your design into sections for construction. "Colourwash Checker-board" (page 17) is made up of nine blocks plus a border three squares wide. "Log Cabin Colourwash" (pages 68 and 99) consists of nine blocks and a border two squares wide. "Colourwash Stripes I" (at right), divided not into the lozenge shapes you see but into two simple mirror-image blocks and two border blocks, which are also mirror images of each other.

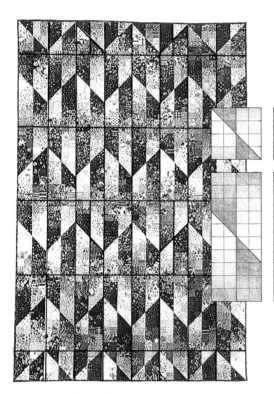

Colourwash Stripes I, *showing the four blocks used to make the quilt.*

Colourwash Stripes I *by Deirdre Amsden, 1987, Cambridge, England, 57" x 86". Machine pieced from 1³/₄" squares and right-angled triangles. This was my first large-scale quilt using an assortment of printed fabrics. (See design sketches on page 46.)*

On the other hand, "Colourwash Diamonds" (right and in color on page 119) did not break down neatly along design elements. I found it best to divide it into large diamond sections regardless of the design. Some designs, such as the Colourwash Cubes quilts on page 77, cannot be divided into sections because they have no long, continuous seams. (See "Half Seams" on page 112.)

Colourwash Diamonds, *showing the overall design divided into sections for piecing.*

DESIGN ETIQUETTE

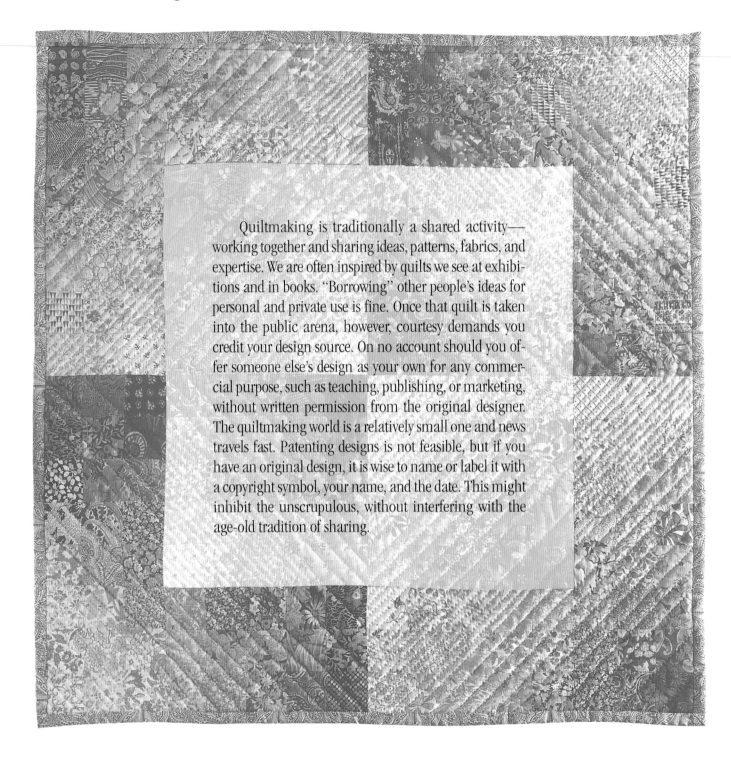

Quiltmaking is traditionally a shared activity—working together and sharing ideas, patterns, fabrics, and expertise. We are often inspired by quilts we see at exhibitions and in books. "Borrowing" other people's ideas for personal and private use is fine. Once that quilt is taken into the public arena, however, courtesy demands you credit your design source. On no account should you offer someone else's design as your own for any commercial purpose, such as teaching, publishing, or marketing, without written permission from the original designer. The quiltmaking world is a relatively small one and news travels fast. Patenting designs is not feasible, but if you have an original design, it is wise to name or label it with a copyright symbol, your name, and the date. This might inhibit the unscrupulous, without interfering with the age-old tradition of sharing.

COLOR

There are no rules about color, although people have tried to make them from time to time. I remember a line from an absurd childhood rhyme: "Blue and green should never be seen." Color theory, color wheels, and the language we employ to talk about color help us use, communicate, and think about color, but they are not rules. Feel free to use color however you wish. Some people seem to have a natural flair for grouping colors. Most of us have to work at it. Luckily, playing with color and colored fabrics is enjoyable, and the end results will be no worse for the time, thought, and effort expended.

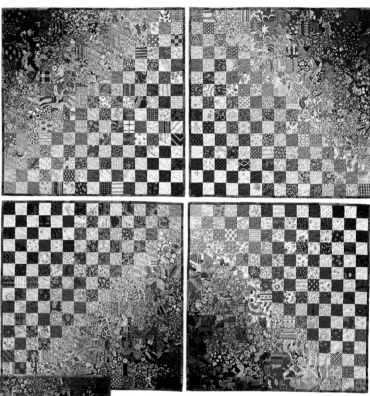

Colouration 1, 2, 3, & 4 by Deirdre Amsden, 1992, London, England, four sections each measuring 24" x 24". This quilt is a larger-scale version of "The Four Seasons" on page 25. However, here color provides the transition from one piece to the other. The sections move from an achromatic arrangement (no color) through cool and warm to a bright polychromatic arrangement of colors.

Glossary

Color: a sensation of light induced by electromagnetic waves of a certain frequency. The frequency determines the color we see. The eye is constantly trying to simplify and create order in color and prefers precise colors.

Hue: the name we use to identify a color, such as blue, red, or yellow.

Intensity, saturation, chroma: the strength or purity of a color. A saturated color is one of maximum strength and purity and contains no gray.

Value: the degree of lightness or darkness of a color.

Tint: a color mixed with white, which makes it lighter and higher in value.

Tone: a color mixed with gray (or with its complement as described at right), which changes its intensity.

Shade: a color mixed with black, which makes it darker and lower in value.

Primary colors: the colors from which all other colors are derived. Primary colors differ according to the medium you are using. (See below.)

Secondary colors: mixtures of two adjacent primary colors. (See the color wheel on page 52.)

Intermediate colors: mixtures of adjacent primary and secondary colors.

Tertiary colors: mixtures of two secondary colors.

Color wheel: an arrangement of colors in a circle with primary, secondary, and intermediate colors displayed in order.

Monochromatic color harmony: harmony of one color and its tints, tones, and shades (not to be confused with monotone which means sameness of color). "Night-time Blues" (page 107) is a good example of monochromatic harmony.

Analogous color harmony: harmony of related colors (those adjacent to each other on the color wheel).

Complementary color harmony: harmony of contrasting colors (those colors opposite each other on the color wheel). The strongest of these harmonies is between two colors directly opposite each other. A complementary color works well as an accent color to enliven an analogous color harmony.

Pigment: Yellow, red, and blue are the three colors that cannot be created by mixing. These colors form the basis of the artists' and dyers' color wheel.

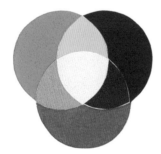

Light: Red, blue-violet, and green are the primary colors of light. When all three are mixed together, they form white light. Television uses the primary colors of light.

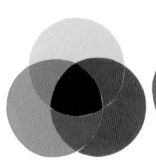

Process printing: Printing and platemaking use the primary colors of both pigment and light. The yellow (zanth) plate is made by photographing the image to be printed through a blue filter, the magenta (achlor) through a green filter, and the blue (cyan) through a red filter.

Perception: There are four visual elementary colors: yellow, red, blue, and green. Green is not a primary color in the pigment sense, but visually it has equal status with yellow, red, and blue.

Achromatic harmony: harmony without color (black, white, and gray). Using a saturated color with an achromatic harmony can be very dramatic.

Polychromatic harmony: multicolored harmony.

Rainbow harmony: harmony that uses the six colors of the spectrum: red, orange, yellow, green, blue, and violet.

Warm colors: those colors containing red or yellow.

Cool colors: those colors containing blue or green. Warm colors attract the eye, and we can see more warm colors than cool ones because the lenses of our eyes have a yellowish tinge.

Warm and cool colors are relative. A blue containing red looks warm next to a blue containing green, even though blues are cool in relation to warm colors, such as red and orange.

Receding colors: dark, dull, cool colors. These colors appear to recede.

Advancing colors: light, bright, warm colors. These colors appear to advance.

Bright, light and large to the fore with dull, dark, and small receding.

Bright, light and small to the fore with dull, dark, and large receding.

Bright, strong, and large to the fore with dull, pale, and small receding into the mist.

A sense of space is created by using color, value, scale (of prints and size of the squares) and the positioning of the squares.

The Color Wheel

For a long time, I have considered green to be as visually important as yellow, red, and blue. My opinion was recently affirmed when I read that Leonardo da Vinci also considered green (as well as black and white) to be equally important in painting as were yellow, red, and blue. I then found references to the work of the Scandinavian Color Institute in Stockholm. Dr. Anders Hard of the institute has devised a system of color notation called the "Natural Color System." The color wheel of the NCS is based on the four colors they call the elementary colors: yellow, red, blue, and green.

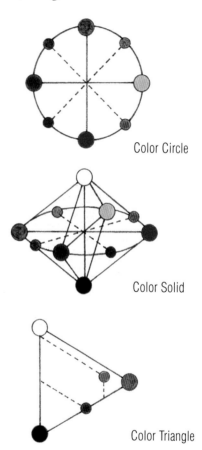

Color Circle

Color Solid

Color Triangle

The Swedish Natural Color System

The NCS is a logical color system based on how human beings see color and six pure colors: white, black, yellow, red, blue, and green (the elementary colors). The colors are arranged in a twin cone shape (color solid), which separates into a circle of forty pure colors of maximum intensity and forty triangles. Black, white, and one of the pure colors form the three points of each triangle. The tints, tones, and shades relating to that pure color are positioned within the triangle.

I have based the color wheel in this book on these four colors, plus black and white, because unless you are dyeing your own fabric, you are making visual color choices when you choose fabrics for quilts.

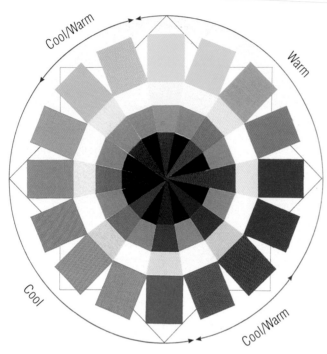

Color wheel based on the four visual elementary colors: yellow, red, blue, and green, placed at the four points of the compass. It also illustrates the four secondary colors— orange, violet, blue-green (turquoise), and yellow-green (lime)— and the eight intermediate colors. Shades (mixed with black), tones (mixed with gray), and tints (mixed with white) for the four elementary and four secondary colors are also illustrated.

Color Responses

Our response to color is emotional rather than intellectual. Colors affect our moods and feelings, which in turn determine our response to colors. We all see colors slightly differently.

Our emotional response to color inspires various color associations, and colors acquire symbolic meanings that differ from culture to culture. Color is a language with which we can convey all sorts of messages. Indeed, color sensations can be so powerful as to play tricks on our other senses, especially taste. Advertisers and retailers use this knowledge to seduce us and influence our purchasing habits. They spend a great deal on market research and put a lot of thought into color. This makes advertisements an excellent source for color ideas. Other obvious sources are paintings and the natural world. (See Color Exercise Two on page 54.)

Because we respond emotionally to color, we can be manipulated and encouraged to change our preferences. We are not consistent when it comes to choosing colors. Sometimes we choose by preference, sometimes we are influenced by fashion, and at other times by mood. Colors themselves are also inconsistent. They are affected by time of day, amount and type of light, adjacent colors, and surrounding colors. I have a red kilim (a woven rug), which has a pattern in off-white, black, and yellow. The yellow glows during the day, but under artificial light it disappears completely, and the whole design changes.

Using Color

Beginning quiltmakers are often unsure about color. They labor under the misconception that the fewer colors they use, the easier it will be. Actually, the opposite is true. When working with a limited range of colors, it is important to get the relationship and balance right to make them work well together. *The more colors you add, the less significant each individual color becomes.* When you work with a lot of colors, however, you need to put more thought into value, contrast, and accent colors. A quick glance at the quilts in this book reveals that I more often than not use all the colors I can lay my hands on. I do not select colors so much as decide where to place them.

The keys to learning about and using color are observing and playing. American knitter and color evangelist Kaffe Fassett says, "a sense of color is not something you automatically know about; you discover and rediscover its secrets by playing with it and, above all, by constantly looking." (See Color Exercise Five on page 54 and Color Excercise Nine on page 55.)

Fabric Color

If selecting fabrics for a quilt were just a decision about color, then any type of fabric would do as long as the color was right. However, the type of fabric has to be as right as the color. This makes color choices more complex. In addition to color, you need to consider the weight, weave, fiber content, and finish of a fabric. How it will handle and its compatibility with the other fabrics are also important factors. Though the colors match, red satin looks and feels very different from red velvet.

Prints give us an even greater range of colors from which to choose. To use red as an example, black printed on red produces a shade that is akin to red paint mixed with black. Red printed on white results in a tint, and when you print another color on red, its redness changes. In addition, the way colors are distributed within the print can create different visual textures.

When you consider how many new printed fabrics are produced each season, the choice seems unlimited. The best way to make color decisions is to experiment. Use the color wheel and the exercises beginning on page 54 to build your confidence. It is just a matter of practice and experience—playing around until something interesting and exciting happens. No amount of color theory is going to persuade you to like yellow if you detest it, but experimenting may reveal ways of using it to advantage in your quilts.

HUES

SHADES

TINTS

TONES

Hues, tints, tones, and shades illustrated in fabric

Color Exercises

At first glance, some of these exercises may not seem immediately relevant to Colourwash arrangements. They are designed to build color confidence and to start beginners thinking about color, which is helpful for any style of quiltmaking. Pick out the exercises you think will help you most.

To carry out the following warm-up exercises, you will first need to gather some color samples or swatches. I have done this by collecting paint color cards, gift wrap papers, and snippets of fabric. Try not to select colors at this stage. Just collect any and every color and value regardless of your likes and dislikes—even the indeterminate, sludgy, and garish ones.

> ### Note
>
> Exercises Six and Seven are the most helpful for Colourwash quilts. As discussed in the chapter on design, values define your design, and eventually you will need to sort your patches according to their value. You will find some tips for checking tonal values on page 74.

Color Exercise One: Sort all your color swatches (both plain and patterned) into one of four piles according to their predominant color: yellow, red, blue, or green. If you have a gray swatch, decide if it is a yellow/gray, pink/gray, blue/gray, or green/gray. (On the off chance that it is a pure gray, put it with the pure blacks and whites.) Now attempt a further subdivision of each pile into warm and cool, such as warm reds and cool reds.

Color Exercise Two: Find a picture in a magazine with colors that appeal to you and pick out swatches that match the colors in the picture. Try to reflect not only the colors but also their values and the quantity of each color. This is very important when using color. The color relationship can change if the relative amounts change. Until you gain confidence with color, this is a good way to select colors. You may find it useful to use a "window" (page 20) to isolate a group of colors in your picture. Now try translating some of these color choices into fabric by making sample blocks.

Color Exercise Three: If you have strong prejudices against certain colors, especially bright ones, pick them out of your swatches. Take one at a time and add other colors to it. Try to make the disliked color essential to the color scheme so that the whole scheme suffers when you remove it.

We often dislike a color because it is used inappropriately. The color is not wrong; it is just in the wrong place. The local authority for the part of London where I live chose to paint the street furniture either acid lime green or purple. It would be hard to imagine two colors less appropriate to the cityscape of streets, houses, and parks. Perhaps that was the idea, but it is certainly painful to live with the result.

Color Exercise Four: Select a color at random and describe it as precisely as you can in terms of purity of hue, value, temperature, associations, and comparisons, as if you were describing it to someone over the telephone. This is a good game to play with a partner, who can judge how well you do when you reveal the color.

Now think of both an appropriate and an inappropriate use for this color.

Color Exercise Five: With the help of the color wheel, group colors into the harmonies listed in the glossary at the beginning of this chapter. Use a variety of tints, tones, and shades as well as pure colors to give value contrasts within the harmonies. Now try giving them a warm, cool, light, dark, bright, or muted overtone. You could also make up sample blocks to try out the harmonies that appeal to you.

Color Exercise Six: Divide your swatches into two piles according to whether they are dark or light in value. Now try the same exercise, but this time make three value piles: dark, medium, and light. Then try dividing them into four values: very dark, medium-dark, medium-light, and very light.

Color Exercise Seven: Make a value scale. This is perhaps the most difficult of all the exercises, so start by selecting one color and pick out all the tints, tones, and shades of that color. Arrange them in order from darkest to lightest.

Now try the same thing with a completely random selection of colors. Include some really strong, pure, bright colors as well as some muted, neutral ones. Try to find each color's correct place in the value scale. Concentrate on their lightness or darkness, not their hue. It is quite difficult to disregard color. You might find the gray scale on page 143 helpful in determining the value of a color. Move the color in question along the scale until one of the grays and the color seem to balance or match. This should give you some idea of its position in your value scale. You will probably find some of the bright colors, especially pure yellow and orange, difficult to place. Although the pure hues in the color wheel are saturated colors, they do not all have the same value. Yellow is much higher in value than red or violet.

Color Exercise Eight: Lay a pale-colored filter or sheet of cellophane over a random selection of colored swatches. Then from your main pile of swatches, pick out colors that match the first swatches as they appear through the filter. Remove the colored cellophane from your random selection and compare the two groups. The second group should be more harmonious, but you may feel it needs an extra spark. You can create the same effect by dyeing different fabrics in the same dye bath (See "Overdyeing" on page 61).

Color Exercise Nine: Adapt Roger Coleman's suggestion (page 21) for increasing visual awareness to color awareness. Instead of looking for shapes and patterns, look at colors as you walk down the street. Concentrate, perhaps, on one color and its variations. Young children are good at playing this sort of game, especially on car trips. Play it together. While you learn to observe, you can help a young child learn to recognize and talk about color.

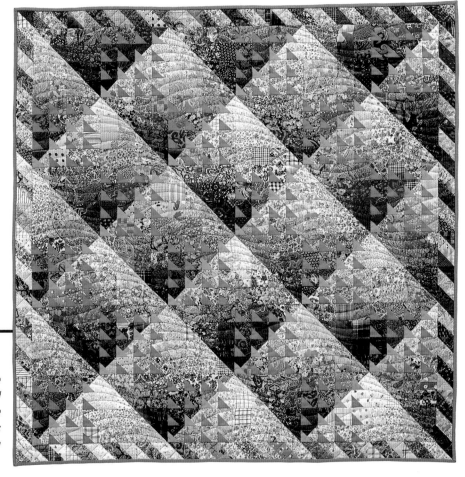

Colourwash Diamonds and Green Triangles by Deirdre Amsden, 1992, London, England, 52" x 52". Machine pieced from 2" squares and right-angled triangles of soft wool/cotton twill-weave fabrics. The brightly colored triangles seem to float above the Colourwash pattern and the undulating quilting.

FABRICS FOR COLOURWASH

Colourwash Cuboids and Pink Triangles *by Deirdre Amsden, 1992, London, England, 69" x 57". Machine pieced from 2" squares and right-angled triangles. The cuboid shapes are seen through a flicker of brightly colored triangles. The border triangles echo the bright triangles in the center.*

"*Because they knew each other's thoughts, they even quarreled without speaking. And sometimes—perhaps after one of these silent quarrels, when they needed their mother to unite them—they would stand over her patchwork quilt and peer at the black velvet stars and the hexagons of printed calico that had once been her dresses. And without saying a word they would see her again—in pink, walking through the oatfield with a jug of draught cider for the reapers. Or in green at a sheep-shearers' lunch. Or in a blue-striped apron bending over the fire. But the black stars brought back a memory of their father's coffin, laid out on the kitchen table, and the chalk-faced women, crying."*

From *On the Black Hill* by Bruce Chatwin

Fabric plays a significant role in all our lives. We handle cloth every day. We use it to adorn our bodies and our homes, and to a great extent, others judge us by how we do this. From cradle to grave, we associate our workaday lives and special occasions with fabrics. And, as the quotation above describes, they can evoke memories as vividly as any smell or sound. It is because quilts are stitched from cloth that they have a special appeal.

Collecting Fabrics for Colourwash

Perhaps the habit of fabric collecting deserves study. I had a collection of fabric long before I took up quiltmaking. At school, I made a book of swatches categorized by fiber content. Once, in the sixties, we thought we might emigrate to America. I packed my trunk with fabric and a sewing machine. The sewing machine would only work with an adapter, and why did I think I wouldn't be able to buy fabric in America?

I try to regard my collection rationally, but when a favorite fabric is running out, I sew tiny pieces together to make one last square. My mother is just the opposite. She feels she must use up her collection and not be left with any fabric. She actually manages this from time to time! My mother would love to be let loose among my fabrics because she worries I'll never use them all without her help. Other people buy fabric with no intention of ever using it because it is just too beautiful to cut up. My sister gave me just such a piece one Christmas.

Although I am attracted to and love patterned fabrics, my designs do not rely on particular prints. When they are cut into small pieces, prints lose some of their identity and when put together with many other prints, they are transformed into a new irregular patterning.

The regular pattern repeat is disturbed when a print is cut into small squares and repieced into a different arrangement.

A variety of prints form an irregular patterning.

I collect any and every type of print and fabric. However, I group them by compatibility in a quilt. Matching quality, fiber, and weave helps in the illusion of creating a whole piece of cloth from small patches.

A. Colourwash Framed VIII, detail showing small-scale prints used for a miniature. (See page 145 for whole quilt.)

B. Colourwash Stripes II, detail showing wool/cotton mixture in a twill weave. (See page 24 for whole quilt.)

C. Colourwash Overlay III, detail showing Liberty Tana lawn. (See page 8 for whole quilt.)

D. Colourwash Stripes III, detail showing assorted dress-weight cottons and lightweight furnishing fabrics. (See page 66 for whole quilt.)

The beauty of collecting fabrics for Colourwash quilts is that even small scraps are useful. Quiltmaking's tradition of thrift plays a significant role in my work and its development. I love to use fabric that might otherwise be discarded. However, I do buy short lengths of fabric frequently to update my palette.

I spend quite a lot of time browsing in fabric stores getting to know fabrics, feeling them, reading the labels for fiber content, country of origin, and care instructions, and checking out trends and fashions. Quilt specialty stores understand quilters. Find a store that has interesting and unusual fabrics, gives swatches for matching purposes, and is happy to cut small pieces from the bolt. If you spend lots of time in your favorite shop, be sure to let the staff know what you want. They may not be able to oblige on every count, but they will get a feel for your needs. Fashion fabrics often have a very short shelf life, so buy them when you see them.

If you are searching for variety, as I always am, there are other places to find fabrics. Garment makers and tailors are sometimes glad to be rid of their remnants. Thrift shops and rummage or garage sales can be good hunting grounds, but you must be strict with yourself and avoid fabric weakened by wear, washing, sunlight, dampness, or insects, however tempting the design. Factory outlets, sales, and discounted remnants can also help stretch your budget. If you are lucky enough to travel abroad, take time to explore markets and search out fabric shops.

When you are shopping with a purpose and looking for a particular color, carry swatches to match. In her book *Color and Cloth*, Mary Coyne Penders recommends using a "window" (page 20). It is sometimes difficult to imagine how fabric on the bolt will look cut into small patches. Isolating a patch by holding a "window" against the fabric helps you visualize it. Another important test is to look at fabrics from a distance. Print fabrics often change in appearance when viewed from afar, and quilts, whether made for beds or walls, are seen both close up and from a distance.

Value, Scale, Color, and Texture

For Colourwash, you need a variety of values, print scales, and colors to give your collection of printed fabrics visual texture.

Value: A good variety of light, medium, and dark fabrics is essential. Don't overlook value in the excitement of selecting colors and prints. The two extremes of very dark and very light fabrics are often in shorter supply than are medium values. Consciously search for these.

Scale: Large-scale prints can be used with small-scale shapes, but it is not as easy to effect a good blend using very small-scale prints and large-scale shapes.

Compare the visual texture of "Sunshine and Shadow" on page 12 with "Sunrise and Sunset" on page 144. Both pieces have small-scale shapes but very different-scale prints. Also compare "Colourwash Stripes and Blue Triangles" on page 96 with "Colourwash Stripe III" on page 126. The visual texture of the smaller quilt is in keeping with its overall size as is true of the bolder texture of the larger quilt.

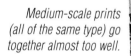

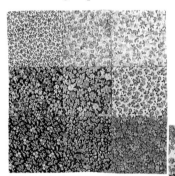

Small-scale prints, which from a distance can act like solids, are more difficult to blend using large-scale shapes.

Medium-scale prints (all of the same type) go together almost too well.

Large-scale prints add visual texture but can be distracting if used too liberally.

Color: It is easy enough to buy colors that you like, but don't restrict your palette by overlooking colors you dislike. There is no point in buying fabric that you really hate, but remember that the fabrics will be cut into small pieces. Colourwash can transform even ugly fabrics. It is surprising how useful they can be for creating an interesting texture or making a transition. Indeed, I have learned to love many of my ugliest fabrics.

Compare your collection of fabrics to the color wheel to discover which colors you lack. Intense, saturated, pure colors may seem overpowering, but don't shy away from them. They light up more sober colors, and you only need small amounts. A little yellow can go an awfully long way. The best way to introduce strong colors is in prints containing other colors.

Texture: I am sometimes asked why I use prints. The truth is that plain fabrics lack visual texture for me. I love the variety you get with prints. They create unexpected juxtapositions and make shading from one value or color to another easier. This variety of visual texture is as vital to Colourwash as a range of values. Your collection should contain as many different prints as possible.

Pattern Types

As shown on page 60, there is a great variety of printed fabrics, and therefore visual textures, from which to choose for quiltmaking.

Monocolored prints: One color printed onto plain cloth. These prints can appear to be almost plain or strongly contrasting, as in the black-and-white check shown in example "A" on page 60. Both extremes can be difficult to blend. However, the first is useful for creating contrast (see the checkerboard areas of "Colouration 1, 2, 3, and 4" on page 49), and the second can provide visual texture.

Multicolored prints: Any print containing more than one color. These are easier to blend than monocolored prints.

Floral prints: There is always an abundance of florals of all types and scales. They are the easiest to blend.

Geometric prints: Stripes, checks, and geometric motifs.

Regular repeats: Motifs repeated at regular intervals, for example spots (dots) and sprigs.

Allover prints: The pattern covers the background uniformly, not in clusters.

Formal and stylized patterns: Paisley patterns are an example of these.

Novelty prints: Prints of animals, maps, words, nursery rhymes, cartoon characters, etc.

Directional prints: Those in which the motifs move or point in one direction.

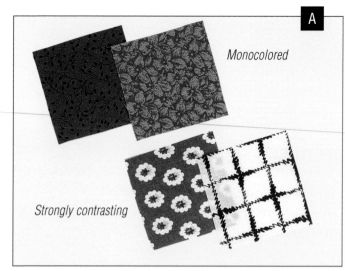

A. Monocolored prints and strongly contrasting prints are difficult but not impossible to use in Colourwash.

B. Floral and multicolored prints.

C. Mixing patterns gives visual texture.

Fabric Preparation

To date, I have made most of my quilts from washable fabrics. I prewash all my fabrics in preparation for sewing. This prevents shrinkage, a worry if the quilt is to be washed. Fabrics shrink at different rates, and even the same fabric can shrink unevenly. Colourwash requires such a variety of fabrics that I would not omit this step.

I wash second-hand fabrics in the washing machine as soon as they come into my possession so they are clean when I put them away. I do not use detergent when washing new fabrics unless they contain a lot of sizing (the chemical finish applied to fabric to give it body).

I sort all new fabrics into dark, medium, and light or into strong colors, such as blues and reds. I then rinse them by hand in water that is as hot as I can bear while wearing household gloves. I rinse them until the water runs clear (at least twice). I remove any fabrics whose dyes violently and continually discolor the water and put them to one side to deal with later. I gently squeeze out the excess water and either roll the wet fabrics in a clean towel or give them a very short spin in the dryer. I then press them while they are still damp. This brings them back to a crisp state. At this stage, I trim off selvages and mark or cut away any flaws, staple holes, or old stitching lines. I sort them by value and keep them in plastic boxes covered with a clean cloth under my work table until I am ready to mark and cut them.

I take the fabrics with unstable dyes, wash them in hot water again, this time with detergent, rinse them until the water runs clear, and press them dry. I then wash them again in detergent, and if the dye runs this time, I banish the fabric to my reject bag. If the rinse water during the first wash really won't run clear, or the fabric leaves dye on the ironing board when I press it, then I discard it without further ado.

Storage

Ideally, fabrics should be stored at room temperature, in dry conditions, and away from direct light. Try to keep your fabric dust-free, but don't resort to air-tight plastic bags or trunks. If you store fabric in cardboard boxes or on wooden shelves, line them with acid-free tissue paper or wrap the fabric in clean cloth.

If your fabric collection is extensive, I suggest you categorize your fabrics for easy access. Sorting by color may work for most quiltmakers, but it is not relevant to Colourwash quilts.

I prefer to store fabrics by type and/or value. I store lengths of fabric for backings in their pristine state, divided into darks, mediums, and lights. I store smaller pieces by type: dress-weight cotton and lightweight furnishing fabrics, twill-weave fabrics, shirtings, Liberty Tana lawn, silks, woolens, and so on. As most of my fabrics are scraps that are difficult to fold, I roll them into bundles by patterns and colorways.

I find it difficult to throw away even the tiniest scrap of fabric. Pieces that are too small for my larger quilts go into a rummage bag, which I raid for miniature quilts and mosaic patchwork. Scraps from these projects, along with thread ends, go into a plastic bag beside my sewing machine. Eventually, when that is full, I steel myself to throw it away.

Extending Your Fabric Palette

I am not fond of dyeing, but from time to time I overdye or tea-dye fabrics that are not useful due to their colors or to strong contrasts that need to be toned down. If the results are disappointing, not too much has been sacrificed. Overdyeing a variety of fabrics is one method of bringing them into harmony.

Overdyeing: I use a commercial brand of dye that is colorfast, simple to use, and does not require boiling. To obtain even color, begin with clean, wet fabric and agitate it frequently throughout the dyeing. Some interesting, if unpredictable, results can be obtained by dyeing crumpled, twisted, knotted, pleated, or folded fabric. Bind the fabric with thread to hold it in place while it soaks, undisturbed, in the dye bath.

Tea dyeing: Soaking fabric in tea can soften the glare of a stark white background. Some fabrics stain more darkly than others, and some emerge looking merely grubby; it is difficult to predict the result. Also be aware that the tannin in tea may damage the fabric over time.

1. Brew a strong pot of loose tea and strain it into a large saucepan, diluting to the required strength; or boil 2–4 tea bags (depending on the color you require and the size of your saucepan) and remove them before immersing the fabric.
2. Put clean, damp fabric into the tea and simmer for 10–30 minutes, gently agitating fabric all the while.
3. Rinse out the surplus tea.
4. Wash and rinse the fabric thoroughly and press while still damp.

Before you overdye or tea-dye a large amount of fabric, or anytime you need to know the end result, experiment with sample swatches. Take detailed notes and complete the dyeing process through to the final pressing. This way, you can see the effect before committing the whole piece of fabric to the dye bath.

Fabric paint: I sometimes paint fabric rather than dye it. Fabric paints are versatile and easy to use. They can be diluted with water, and once dry, they can be fixed with a hot iron. Be sure to buy the correct paint for the type of fabric you are using.

1. Wash new fabric to remove any sizing.
2. Gently stretch the fabric on a board over several layers of absorbent paper. For soft watercolor effects, dampen the fabric and dilute the paint with water. For opaque colors, use undiluted paint on dry fabric. (Opaque pastel colors may be obtained by mixing the manufacturer's medium with the paints without thinning their consistency).
3. Apply the paint with a soft brush, or with a coarse one for visible brush strokes. Applying the paint with a textured sponge or wadded paper also produces interesting effects.

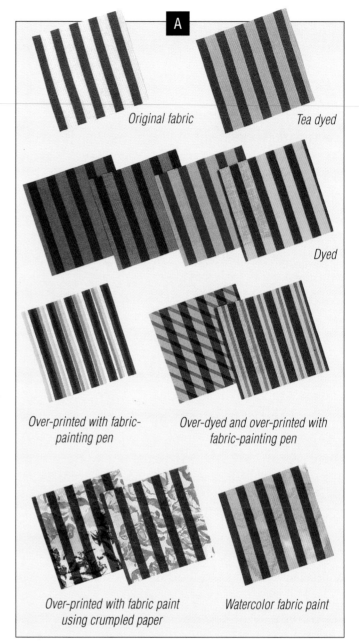

Original fabric   Tea dyed

Dyed

Over-printed with fabric-painting pen

Over-dyed and over-printed with fabric-painting pen

Over-printed with fabric paint using crumpled paper

Watercolor fabric paint

A and B. Two strongly contrasting prints (blue-and-white stripe and stylized flowers) overdyed and overprinted in a number of different ways. Note how the striped fabric took up the dyes more strongly than the stylized print. The overprinting using tightly crumpled paper as a stamp works well on both prints but particularly on the sylized flower. (Fabric-painting pens are fixed with a hot iron in the same way fabric paints are.)

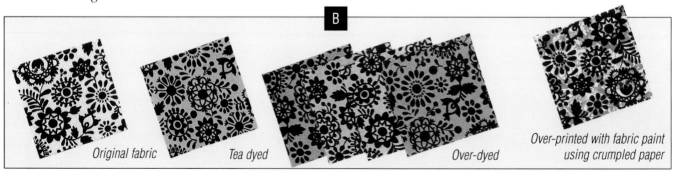

Original fabric   Tea dyed   Over-dyed   Over-printed with fabric paint using crumpled paper

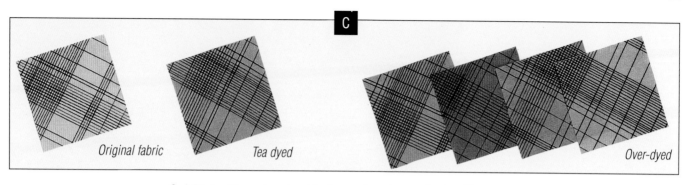

C. A fabric with a pale-colored background can be overdyed, making different colorways—a useful treatment if you have a quantity of the same fabric.

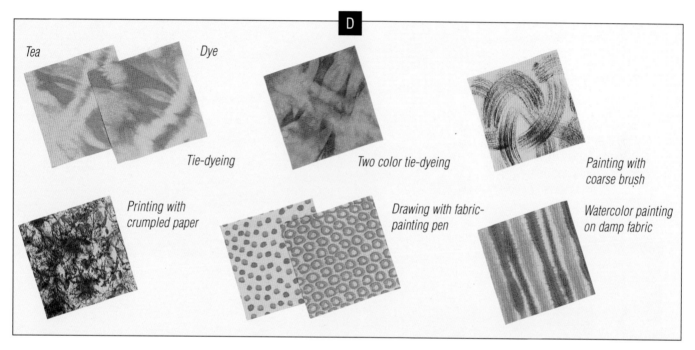

D. Plain fabric (yellow) patterned with tie-dyeing, painting, drawing, and printing.

E. A variety of fabrics brought into harmony by overdyeing in the same dye.

Wear old clothes and a large plastic apron when using dyes and paints. Protect your hands with household gloves, and cover work surfaces with plastic sheeting. Work in a well-ventilated area away from food. Mix and dilute dyes and paints in disposable plastic containers, not bowls or pitchers that you use for cooking, because dye gets into tiny cracks in the glaze. Also protect your ironing board cover with a protective layer of cloth when fixing fabric paints or pressing newly dyed fabric.

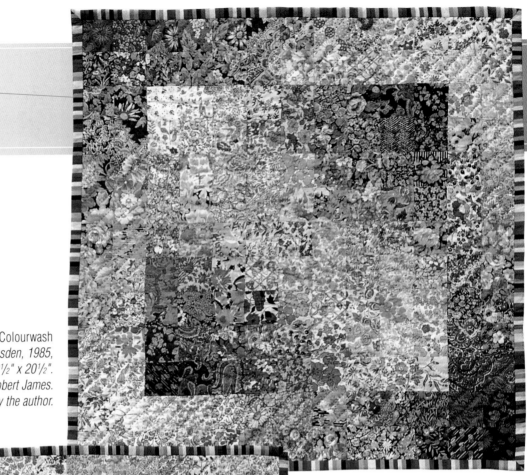

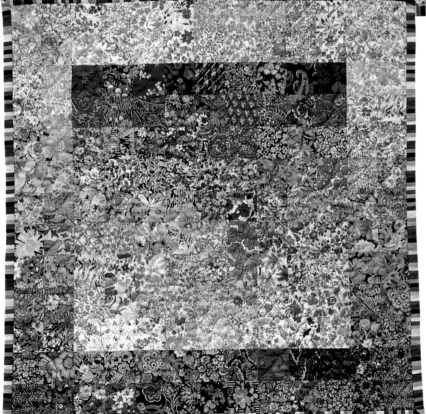

Colourwash Framed I and Colourwash Framed II *by Deirdre Amsden, 1985, Cambridge, England, 20½" x 20½". Collection of Ardis and Robert James. Photograph by the author.*

Colourwash Stripe I by Deirdre Amsden, 1985, Cambridge, England, 22" x 22".
Private collection. Photograph by the author.

From Design to Fabric

This is the moment of transformation when your ideas and design drawings start to take shape. At this stage you are essentially still designing. Your design drawings are not etched in tablets of stone, so be receptive to change if a better idea occurs to you as you work.

Colourwash Stripes III *by Deirdre Amsden, 1990, London, England, 48" x 80". The stripes are cut across by two different angles, creating the illusion of looking through bars to rhomboid shapes beyond. I hand quilted, following the direction of one angle, and machine quilted, following the other. (See page 69 for details of template shapes.)*

The following items are useful for arranging fabric shapes:

Vertical Flannel Board: I made mine from two sheets of soft pin-board (Homosote™) screwed to the wall. I stretched an unbleached, double-sized flannel sheet (83" x 94") over these. Any material with a fuzzy surface would work equally well. I had doubts about how well a flannel board would work and resisted making one for a long time. I dreaded coming into my studio and finding the little patches in a heap on the floor, but my misgivings were unfounded and I would not return to working horizontally on a table. However, if you have no alternative but to work on a table, avoid a highly polished one as the patches will slip and slide on the surface.

Tablecloth Clips: See "Laying Out Your Palette of Patches" on page 71.

Reducing Glass (opposite of a magnifying glass): Use to provide a distanced view of your work. This is especially useful if you must work on a table. Binoculars used the wrong way round, a door peephole, and a camera viewfinder are all acceptable, but less effective, substitutes.

Mirror Tile: This is another distancing device and one that also gives a reverse image of your work. An ideal studio setup would be a flannel board on one wall with a strategically placed mirror on the opposite wall.

Red Cellophane or Filter (optional): Use to check value placements.

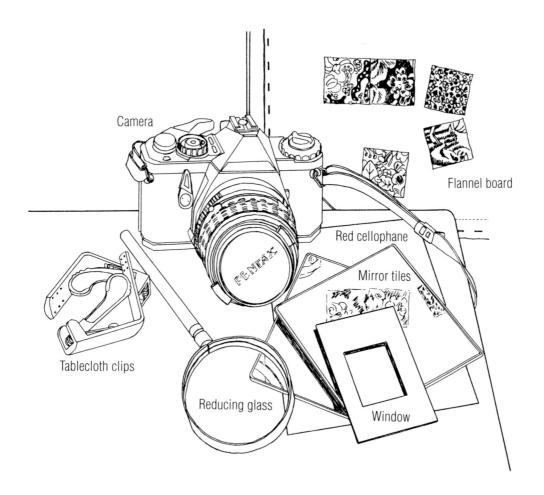

Camera

Flannel board

Red cellophane

Mirror tiles

Tablecloth clips

Reducing glass

Window

MAKING TEMPLATES

Log Cabin Colourwash by Deirdre Amsden, 1990, London, England, 70" x 70". I used the reversible method of Log Cabin for this quilt. It is not quilted. Instructions for making this quilt begin on page 99. Exhibited in New Wave Quilt Collections II, Japan 1992.

Before making templates, recheck your calculations. How big will the quilt be? Do you have enough different fabrics? Although my quilts are not charm quilts (a different fabric for each patch), I try to plan on one fabric for each patch in my design. Then, by the time I have cut duplicates from at least one-fourth of my fabrics, I am fairly certain to have enough patches to carry out my design. You will find that you need many more than the required minimum. Also, you will always have patches left over after making a Colourwash quilt. It is simply unavoidable.

The drawings for "Log Cabin Colourwash" illustrate this process. As you will see from my scribbled calculations, I originally planned 58 squares x 58 squares, which gave me an overall measurement of 87" x 87". This seemed too large, and I didn't think I had enough different fabrics (3,364) to carry out the design. I decided to reduce each block by one strip all around, keeping the template at 1½" square. This gave me a final overall measurement of 69" x 69" and over a thousand fewer fabrics to find. (Compare the initial design drawing at right with the finished quilt above and the amended design drawing on page 99.)

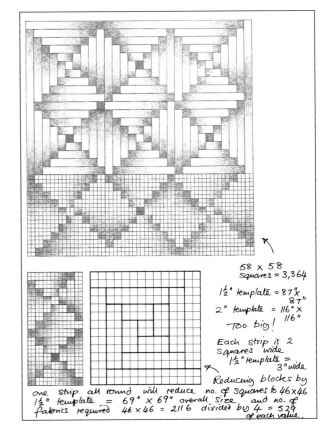

58 x 58
squares = 3,364

1½" template = 87" x 87"

2" template = 116" x 116"
Too big!

Each strip is 2 squares wide
1½" template = 3" wide

Reducing blocks by one strip all round will reduce no. of squares to 46x46
1½" template = 69" x 69" overall size and no. of fabrics required 46x46 = 2116 divided by 4 = 529 of each value.

After deciding on the dimensions of your basic shape or shapes, make an accurate, sturdy template for each one. Study the design drawing for "Colourwash Stripes III" (below). I have enlarged the center section to highlight the five shapes that compose this design. I have drawn out each shape and added the seam allowances. You will notice that, where possible, I have drawn them next to each other to simplify template making. (Complete directions for making templates begin on page 108.)

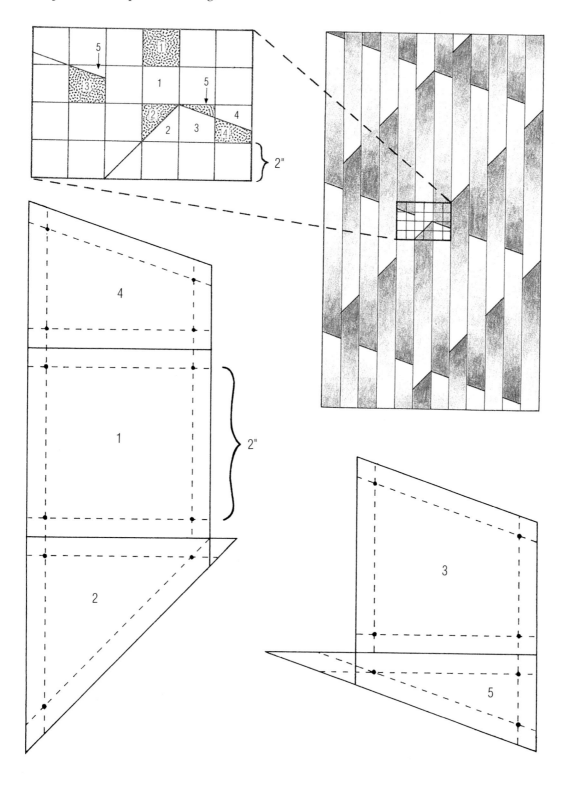

CUTTING TO MAKE THE MOST OF PRINTS

Once you have selected and prepared your fabrics as discussed in the previous chapter, decided upon your method of construction, and made your templates (or decided to rotary cut the shapes), you are ready for the major task of cutting out.

Here are a number of tips for marking and cutting that will make the most of your prints, expand your palette, and yield patches that work best in Colourwash:

- Cut pattern motifs and splashes of color off-center, which enables you to blend one patch into another more easily. To achieve this, place your template so that a motif is cut in half.
- Cut more than one patch out of fabrics that blend easily, and only one patch from difficult or eye-catching prints. Although it provides needed visual texture, if a dazzling print is repeated, the eye tends to dart distractedly from one patch to the other. (See "Pattern Types" on pages 59–60.)
- Cut at least two patches out of directional prints because you can make additional ones look different by turning them.
- If a fabric can double as dark and medium, or light and medium, cut two patches from it, placing one in each of the appropriate value piles.
- Always check the reverse side of a fabric; if you find it interesting, cut an extra patch.
- When you come across a fabric that is lighter in weight than the others, back it with cheesecloth or fine lawn to bring it up to the weight of the other patches. This does not make the lightweight fabric stronger, but it improves its appearance and makes it easier to blend. Mixing fabrics of different weights in a quilt is not generally recommended.

Cut motifs off-center for easier blending.

Directional prints will appear to be different if one is given a quarter turn.

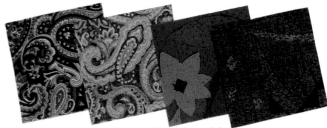

You can often use the right and the wrong side of a fabric in Colourwash.

As you cut out your shapes, sort and stack them in the number of value piles you need for your design. (See "Value" beginning on page 26.) For example, "Colourwash Cubes II" on page 77 took three values (light, medium, and dark), but I used four values (light, medium-light, medium-dark, and dark) for "Checkerboard Colourwash" on page 17.

Day Into Night, *detail of the reverse side of the piecing showing some of the patches lined with cheesecloth. Photograph by the author.*

LAYING OUT YOUR PALETTE OF PATCHES

You will need a large, undisturbed area near your flannel board or work table to lay out your palette of patches. This area should be well lit, but out of direct sunlight, which causes fading. There shouldn't be any drafts from windows, doors, or people moving. I realize not everyone has this type of space. Putting up a flannel board may be relatively easy, but finding space to lay out patches may be more of a problem. For small projects, it can be a temporary space, such as a folding table. As an alternative, lay out your palette on sheets of cardboard. Spread the sheets out on a table while you are working and then cover them with tissue paper and/or cardboard to keep them safe and dust-free and stack away when you finish for the day or need the space. I suggest weighting or clipping the stack together with tablecloth clips to secure it. When you go back to work, take care to lift the sheets of cardboard and tissue paper carefully and slowly so as not to disturb the patches.

The beginning of a striped Colourwash design arranged on the vertical flannel board

1. Start with either the lightest or the darkest pile of patches, and lay them out in rows so that part of each patch is visible. Lay out other value piles in the same way to reveal your whole palette.
2. The design's ratio of lights to darks should be reflected in the palette of patches. "Log Cabin Colourwash" on page 68 required equal quantities of each value. "Night-time Blues" on page 107 had mostly darks, fewer mediums, and even fewer lights. If the proportion in your palette does not correspond to your design, cut more patches of the value(s) you need.

A palette of patches laid out in value groups

CREATING COLOURWASH: GETTING STARTED

Refer to your design drawing to find a logical place to start the arranging process. If you have been able to break your design down into blocks, then it is usually best to start arranging from the center and work outwards. (See "Construction Plan" on page 47.) Other times it is more sensible to start at one edge or corner. I have occasionally started an arrangement in one place only to find that another starting point would have been easier. Sometimes this has meant putting all the patches back into the palette and starting fresh.

If your flannel board (or work table) can accommodate your whole design, you can complete the arrangement before you start sewing. If this is not possible, you will need to arrange and sew the quilt in sections. When I need to work this way, I arrange the first section and leave enough room to arrange part of the adjoining section. I sew the first section together and pin it up over to one side on my flannel board. I then move the prearranged patches of the adjoining section over and continue arranging this section, along with part of the next.

Some designs cannot be divided easily into blocks or sections. "Colourwash Cubes II" and "Colourwash Cubes III" (page 77) and "Night-time Blues" (page 107) had to be arranged in irregular segments.

Blending, Relating, and Contrasting

At last the real moment of truth. All the planning and preparation start to take shape. This stage is like doing a jigsaw puzzle except, unlike a jigsaw puzzle, the patches have no fixed positions. It can be hard to decide which of several patches is the best choice. You need to be decisive, or the process can continue indefinitely. As you become more experienced, you realize that unexpected fabrics work well together and you become more daring in your positioning. Aim for balance and even distribution of color (unless of course your design calls for all the greens in one area and all the reds in another). Also remember the importance of visual texture. It is tempting to ignore all those difficult fabrics, but try to work them in right from the start. Otherwise, you will be left with a lot of difficult fabrics at the end, not to mention uneven visual texture between areas.

Value placements in your design drawing define your design. They are the most important element to interpret into fabric. You need to concentrate on creating a good blend where it is required (avoiding ambiguous "jumps" or "steps") and defining contrasts clearly. Failure on either count leads to confusion and difficulty in interpreting the overall design.

When blending fabrics, try to relate patches not just to their immediate neighbors, but also to patches once or twice removed. Consider the following:

- Color or splashes of color are the most obvious relating device. Pick up the red in one patch and relate it to the red in another, or run a splash of color into a splash of similar color even if the two fabrics are dissimilar in other respects. A fabric containing two colors can act as a go-between in a transition from one color to another.

- A partial motif at the edge of a patch can run into another one, especially if the two relate in some way (shape, color, or size). Surprisingly small marks can be used to effect a blend in this way if they happen to be positioned exactly right. However, remember to take the seam allowance into account. *Sometimes crucial marks or motifs disappear in a seam.*

- Sometimes movement in one patch can be followed through to its neighbor. The eye follows the movement, ignoring the join.

- Occasionally, similar prints may be related even when their colors differ. Stripes, cluster patterns, or like motifs work this way. However, too many similar fabrics together can create a distracting focus.

- Keep patches of the same fabric apart. Also try to avoid putting them next to the same print every time you use them.

As you become more experienced at arranging patches, you will make placement decisions instinctively. Only in hindsight will you realize how you achieved a certain transition.

Similar floral prints blend easily.

Mustard yellow

Blending by color

Blacks, reds, and greens

Off-center motifs

Transition from red to green

Similar prints

Small patch of red

Movement follows through.

Similar shapes

Similar motifs

Similar arrangement of motifs

Checking Your Work

As you work, constantly check to see if the patches are behaving as you want them to. Stand back often to view your work from a distance. I am nearsighted, which has many drawbacks but is a real advantage for this process. Use your reducing glass and also a mirror tile for a reverse image of your arrangement. Replacing a misfit can sometimes be difficult because the replacement has to relate to all the neighboring patches. If I have trouble fitting a replacement into the existing arrangement, I simply remove every patch that came after it and start again from there.

To check value placements, use one of the following techniques for draining away, or neutralizing, color and emphasizing value:

- Red cellophane or a red filter. The Ruby Beholder™ is a tool with a value finder on one end, and a 1½" window template on the other end. Be careful. When viewed through a red filter, red fabrics will appear lighter in value than they really are.
- Half closing (squinting) your eyes.
- Dimming the lights. I often turn my studio lights off the last thing at night and view my work by the light filtering up from downstairs.
- Photocopying. Obviously, you cannot photocopy a whole quilt as you lay it out, but it may prove useful for checking your work for Color Exercises Six and Seven on page 55.

However well you plan, what works on paper does not always work in fabric. Sometimes you may feel things are not going well but you try to ignore it, hoping it will go away. It rarely does, so stop and try to find the problem. There are several strategies that can help you:

- Leave your work for a few hours or days. Come back to it with fresh eyes and a clear head. If you pass your work during the course of the day, you will sometimes come upon it "by surprise" or catch a glimpse of it out of the corner of your eye.
- Look at it upside down. Yes, I mean turn around, bend over, and look at it through your legs!
- Look at your work in a mirror to reverse it and to simulate distance.
- View it through a "window" (page 20) so you can concentrate on the design, masking out any distractions or isolating parts of the design.
- Ask for other people's opinions. They may or may not come up with helpful suggestions, but the discussion might help you clarify your ideas.
- If no one else is around, argue with yourself. Ask yourself questions and try to give honest answers. There is no point in kidding your way through a problem.
- Take photographs for a reduced perspective and an image you can easily rotate and view any way up. You can also cut up and rearrange a photograph.
- Go back to the drawing board.

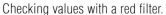

Checking values with a red filter.

Photocopying removes the distraction of color and leaves the values.

Whatever you do, try not to give up until you have explored all avenues. You may well surprise yourself.

Before you begin piecing, test your binding fabric against your arranged design to see if it "works." Also make a final check after the patches are sewn together, just to be sure.

Choosing a binding fabric that achieves the right contrast for a Colourwash quilt can be difficult. Sometimes the answer is to use more than one fabric to contrast with, or echo, the dark/light areas, or to use a bright color. On smaller quilts, I have often found it better to use a print that has not already been used in the patchwork.

Colourwash Cross II by Deirdre Amsden, 1990, London, England, 24½" x 24½". Private collection. Photograph by the author.

Assembling a Colourwash Quilt

You can piece Colourwash quilts by hand or machine. I machine piece because I find it quicker and more accurate.

Accuracy is essential when making a quilt from so many small patches. There are no intermediate points of adjustment as there are in block designs, where it is possible to ease and stretch blocks to fit together. This is why I mark seam lines with a grid ruler. See "Sewing Patches and Matching Seams" on pages 110–11. A few inaccuracies can build up into distortions that cause bulges and wavy edges. I speak from many hair-tearing experiences. Quilting designs that relate to the patchwork shapes provide a further incentive to be accurate. See "Planning the Quilting," beginning on page 43.

Accuracy is especially important when a basic shape is made from two or more smaller shapes. I use a checking template to be sure the basic shape remains accurate as discussed in the construction of the "Colourwash Stripes and Blue Triangles" wall hanging on page 96.

I look at tonal value and basic colors when selecting thread for machine piecing. The colors I find most useful are white or cream, ecru or beige, dark beige or khaki, brown, gray, navy blue, black, mid-blue, mid-green, and red. I like to use extra-fine machine needles: #8 (60) for lawn and #10 (70) for cottons. I change to a #12 (80) when binding a large or heavy quilt.

My sewing machine is a forty-year-old, cast-iron workhorse of a machine. It is good-natured and a superb straight stitcher. It lets me feed the patches through without having to lift the presser foot, and it twists the thread between the patches without tangling. It has never

been serviced (except by me) and has never let me down, but I still dream of the latest high-tech model I will own one day.

I have deliberately placed my machine at the opposite end of my studio from my flannel board, with my work table between the two. This arrangement forces me to move about between stages and gives me constant opportunities to look at my work from a distance.

Once I am happy with the arrangement of patches in either the whole quilt or a section of it, I am ready to begin sewing. I sew the patches into pairs first, then the pairs into blocks of four, then the fours into blocks of eight, and so on. There are fewer seams to match at each stage with this method than there are when sewing patches into long strips and then sewing the strips together. Also, the numerous short seams perpetually crossing the previous ones help to keep them pressed in position. It is only in the final stages of assembly that there are a lot of seams to be matched.

I begin by threading the machine with, say, a light-colored thread and sewing all the light-colored patches together. I then move to the next tonal value, and so on, always sewing in a prearranged sequence so I do not muddle the position of the patches. A thorough description of my sewing methods begins on pages 110. See especially "Colourwash Sewing Sequences" on pages 113–14. The process I outline is unique and essential to Colourwash. As you sew (and take up the seam allowances), the design will begin to fragment. Don't panic—it comes together again at the end, only much smaller.

Colourwash Cubes II
*by Deirdre Amsden, 1990, London,
England, 64" x 52". Collection of
Mr. and Mrs. Thomas R. Maurer.
Photograph by Paul Seheult.*

Colourwash Cubes III *by Deirdre
Amsden, 1990, London, England,
60" x 50". Collection of
Mary E. Simons. Photograph
by Paul Seheult.*

This pair of quilts was commissioned after an exhibition featuring Colourwash Cubes I *(page 137).
I was asked to make two small-scale quilts in a similar style. The solution for reducing the scale of the
cubes came from the quilting design of* Night-time Blues, *a detail of which can be seen on page 41.
I was also asked to sew a sleeve to all four edges so the quilts could be hung up any way.*

Border Assembly

Quilting

I usually make pieced Colourwash borders in sections and add them while piecing the central design. (See "Colourwash Cuboids and Stripes" on page 30 and "Colourwash Cuboids and Pink Triangles" on page 56.) The border is then more likely to fit exactly than it does if I add it as a separate pieced strip. However, sometimes this is unavoidable as in "Log Cabin Colourwash" on page 68, and you need to make sure the borders fit before attaching them. See "Adding the Borders" on page 117.

I love this stage of quiltmaking, when the patchwork starts to come to life and takes on the depth and tactile qualities so characteristic of quilts. When I used to give public demonstrations of quilting, the most common question after "How long does it take?" was "How do you have the patience?" Well, housework, supermarket shopping, and London transport try my patience, not quilting. For me, quilting completes the work of piecing and is an equally engrossing part of the process.

Apart from the practical functions of holding the layers of a quilt together and stabilizing and strengthening pieced patchwork, quilting stitches add pattern and texture. If designed for the purpose, they can also help to disguise seams and blend patches together. (See "Planning the Quilting," beginning on page 43.) Because quilting serves more than a functional purpose, it can be fun to experiment. Thread, batting, and stitches can all be varied to give different quilting effects. (See "Stitch Variations" on pages 124–25.) Also, in contrast to the broken line of hand quilting, the continuous line of machine quilting (pages 125–26) gives an appearance of etched marks across the surface of a quilt.

When hand quilting, I often experiment with thicker threads, such as lace-making thread (Filato di Cantu #30), coton à broder #18, or pearl cotton #8. They are a little harder to thread through a quilting needle, but they are beautiful, soft threads that emphasize my stitches without enlarging them. For finer work, I like Mölnlycke quilting thread or pure silk. There are many other lustrous and metallic threads that invite experimentation.

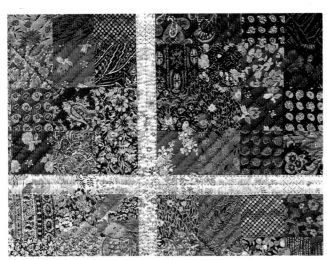

Colourwash Lattice I. *Detail showing whipped quilting done with pearl cotton. (See page 132 for whole quilt and page 125 for instructions.)*

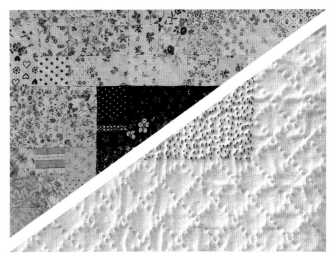

Sunrise and Sunset, *front and back. Details showing stipple quilting done with fine quilting thread. (See page 144 for the whole quilt and page 125 for instructions.)*

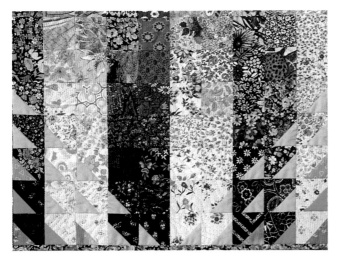

Colourwash Stripes and Blue Triangles. *Detail showing meander quilting done with lace thread. (See page 96 for whole quilt and page 125 for instructions.) Loaned by* Quilt San Diego, *C & T Publications*

Colourwash Stripe III. *Detail showing machine quilting done with transparent nylon filament. (See page 126 for whole quilt. Instructions for machine quilting begin on page 125.)*

I select battings for their compatibility with the fabrics I have used for the patchwork and backing and also for the effect they have on my quilting. Some battings are easier to quilt than others and some require more stitching, but each will give your quilting a different appearance. This depends on their fiber content and the amount of loft. Polyester battings are probably the most versatile, ranging from high to low loft. All- and part-cotton battings can be a little more difficult to quilt and tend to be denser and flatter in appearance. Wool is beautiful to quilt and holds its loft, but the fibers tend to migrate if it is unbonded. Silk batting is just a dream to quilt but may be expensive and hard to find.

I use either a 20" round hoop or a hardwood frame my brother-in-law made for me. It has two rail sizes and sits on chairbacks or a couple of trestles. If you are new to quilting, I suggest you try a hoop. A diameter of 14" to 18" is probably a better size than 20" for a beginner.

I used to baste all my quilts regardless of whether I was using a frame or a hoop. Now I only baste if I am going to quilt in a hoop or by machine. Basting a large quilt is hard work; if possible, enlist the help of a quilter friend whom you can repay in kind. (Basting instructions begin on page 120.)

FINISHING

By the time you reach the finishing stage, enthusiasm may be running low or, more probably, a quilt show deadline may be looming. Don't be hasty or careless at this point; you may ruin your quilt and in the long run won't really save time. Does this sound like the voice of experience speaking? Finishing is as important as all the other processes involved in making a quilt, and good finishing habits pay dividends.

There are two main methods of neatening the edges of a quilt. The first is to encase the raw edges in a binding, either single, double, or self- (where the backing is brought over to the front and stitched down). The second method is to turn in the two raw edges and stitch them together. Piping cord or edgings, such as Prairie Points (page 90), may be inserted between the two edges.

Once your quilt edge is finished, try to find just a bit more time for the final touches—labels, signatures, and hanging sleeves.

Labels and Signatures

Future generations and owners of your quilts will treasure them all the more for a few personal details. I now embroider my name and the year on the front of my quilts, but I still make a label with a few more details for the reverse. I embroider my signature while I am piecing the quilt top, but wait until the quilt is finished before making the label for the back since it includes the month and year it was completed as well as the title and any other relevant details. The more information you can pass on about your quilt, the better. Here are a few ideas: title, date, inspiration, occasion, location, who made it, and for whom. You can either embroider labels or write them with a fabric marking pen. See page 135 for more details.

A variety of ways to finish the edges of Colourwash quilts is shown at left. Clockwise from right: Prairie Points shown on "Crib Quilt for Summer Baby." Instructions begin on page 87. Binding shown on "Colourwash Stripe II," page 4. Piping shown on "Log Cabin Colourwash," page 68. Instructions begin on page 99. Facing shown on "Colourwash Lattice I," page 132.

Hanging Sleeves

A tubular sleeve sewn to the reverse top edge of a quilt is a neat way to hang a quilt for either temporary or permanent display. It conceals the hanging rod and distributes the weight of the quilt evenly for minimum stress. A tubular sleeve also protects the back of the quilt from the hanging rod. Unless they are part of the quilt construction, hanging loops can strain a quilt at the points of attachment.

For temporary display, make a loose sleeve that can be removed. For more permanent display, the sleeve can be made as part of the quilt. A large or heavy quilt requires a sleeve made in two or more sections so the hanging rod can be attached at intervals. (Instructions begin on page 134.)

Be sure to sign or label your quilt.

PART THREE
PROJECTS

The following seven projects cover all skill levels and a variety of techniques. It is difficult to give yardage requirements for Colourwash piecing. You need many more pieces than you will actually use, but precisely how many is difficult to forecast. When I do give amounts, they are for 44"-wide fabric unless otherwise indicated.

Templates are given for each project. They may be traced or copied (not photocopied) onto graph paper marked in a ¼" grid (4 squares to the inch).

COLOURWASH CUSHIONS

Colourwash Cushions *made in 1993
by members of the Cambridge Quilters,
England. Each cushion measures 18" x 18".*

These cushions were made as a "challenge" by The Cambridge Quilters of England. Some members made several cushions, and one went on to develop her cushion into a crib quilt. At the final count, ten people took part and produced a total of sixteen cushions.

Skill Level: Novice

Dimensions: 18" x 18". Each cushion cover is composed of 144 squares, each 1½" finished.

Template: Template #1 (page 86)

Colourwash Cushion *by Deirdre Amsden,
London, England, 18" x 18".*

Shaded design drawing showing a
suggestion for quilting (broken lines).

Materials

Assorted fabrics for the squares*
1 square of lining fabric, 20" x 20"
⅝ yd. fabric for the cushion back**
¼ yd. fabric for binding
Sewing and quilting thread
5 buttons

*Ten people took up the challenge. Each person cut 10 squares (2" x 2") from each of 18 to 20 different fabrics: 6 dark, 6 medium, and 6 light; or 5 dark, 5 medium-dark, 5 medium-light, and 5 light. Each quilter sorted her squares into 10 piles, each of which contained 1 of each fabric, keeping 1 pile for herself and distributing the other 9. Everybody ended up with a total of 180 to 200 different squares, to which they added more of their own.

**I often cut the cushion back from the front of a second-hand shirt as it already has a convenient button opening.

Preparation

1. Make Template #1 (page 86).
2. Wash and press all your fabrics.
3. Mark and cut a square from each of your fabrics and sort into 4 values (dark, medium-dark, medium-light, and light).
4. Lay out your palette (see "Laying Out Your Palette of Patches" on page 71).

Construction

1. Arrange your patches, following the design drawing, on page 84, or substitute one of the other design possibilities below or one of your own designs.

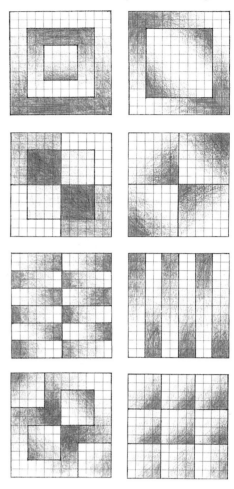

Alternate designs for a cushion cover.

2. When you are happy with the arrangement, sew the patches together, first into pairs, then into sets of four, and so on. Press the seams open as you sew. See "Sewing the Pieces Together," beginning on page 110.
3. To line the completed patchwork, place it right side up on the lining fabric and baste the two together. Trim surplus lining.

Note

If you wish to quilt your cushion cover, first mark the quilting design, then layer the top with batting and lining; baste. Quilt.

4. For the cushion back, cut 2 pieces, each 12¾" x 19", from the backing fabric.
5. On one long edge of each piece, turn under and stitch ¼".

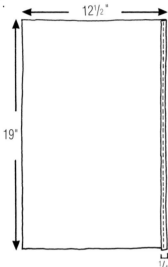

6. Turn under 2" and press. On one of the turned edges, make 5 buttonholes to fit your buttons on the other. Button the pieces together. The back should measure 19" x 19" when buttoned.

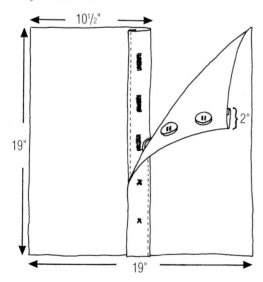

7. Layer the cushion back and top with wrong sides together. Pin and then baste the outer edges together.
8. Cut 2"-wide strips from your binding fabric. Join into a continuous strip long enough to reach around the cushion (about 80"). Fold it in half lengthwise with wrong sides together and press. Bind the edges and miter the corners, referring to "Single-and Double-Layer Binding" on pages 128–32.

Creative Variations

- Adjust the size of your cushion by altering the template size or the number of squares in your design.
- Pipe the outer edges and use a zipper in one seam for the opening instead of the buttoned back. (See "Piping" on page 103.)

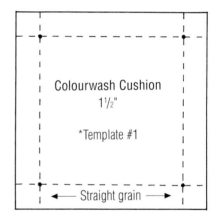

*Use this template for Colourwash Log Cabin on page 99.

CRIB QUILT FOR A SUMMER BABY

Crib Quilt for a Summer Baby *by Deirdre Amsden, 1993, London, England, 24" x 32".*

I used seven different Liberty of London Tana lawn fabrics to make this summer crib quilt and finished it with a Prairie Point edging.

Skill Level: Intermediate

Dimensions: 24" x 32" excluding the edging

Templates: #1, #2, and #3 (page 91)

Materials

7 cotton lawn fabrics (36" or 44" wide) that blend together and range from light to dark: ½ yd. of Fabric #1 (lightest), ½ yd. of Fabric #7 (darkest), and ¼ yd. each of Fabrics #2, #3, #4, #5, and #6
¾ yd. backing fabric
¾ yd. low-loft batting
Sewing and quilting thread

Preparation

1. Make Templates, #1, #2, and #3 (page 91).
2. Wash and press all your fabrics.
3. Cut an 18" x 22" piece from Fabric #1 (lightest fabric) and set aside. Cut 32 triangles (Template #2) from the remainder, making sure to follow the arrow for grain-line placement.
4. Cut 36 squares-on-point (Template #1) from Fabric #2, 40 from Fabric #3, 44 from Fabric #4, 48 from Fabric #5, and 52 from Fabric #6.
5. Cut 56 triangles (Template #2) and 56 Prairie Point squares (Template #3) from Fabric #7 (the darkest fabric).

Construction

1. Make 16 pieced triangles from the 32 triangles (Template #2) cut from Fabric #1 (the lightest) and 16 squares-on-point (Template #1) cut from Fabric #2. Press seams open.

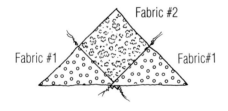

2. Make 28 pieced triangles from the 56 triangles (Template #2) cut from Fabric #7 (the darkest) and 28 squares-on-point (Template #1) cut from Fabric #6. Press seams open.

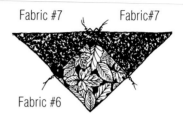

3. Make 20 pieced squares-on-point from the remaining 20 squares-on-point (Template #1) cut from Fabric #2, 40 from Fabric #3, and 20 from Fabric #4. Press seams open.

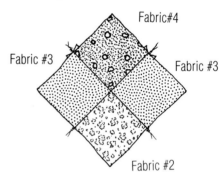

4. Make 24 pieced squares-on-point from the remaining 24 squares-on-point (Template #1) cut from Fabric #4, 48 from Fabric #5, and the remaining 24 from Fabric #6. Press seams open.

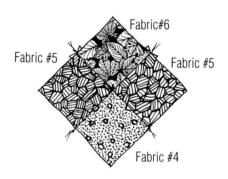

5. From these pieced triangles and squares-on-point, make up 2 of Section A, 2 of Section B, and 4 of Section C. Press seams open. (See design drawing on page 87 and the illustration on the right.)

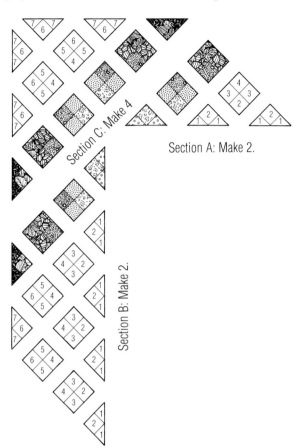

Section A: Make 2.

7. Sew a Section A to opposite ends of the center panel (D) and then add a Section B to the remaining sides. Press seams open.

8. Add a Section C to each corner of the quilt top. Press the seams open.

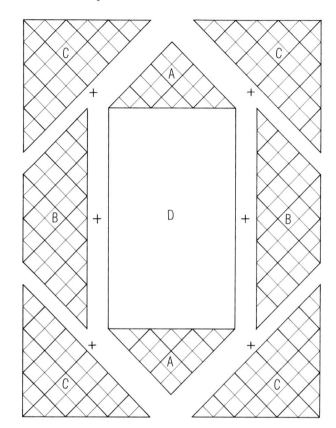

6. Check the measurements of the longest edges of Sections A and B. They should measure 12" and 20", respectively. Cut the center panel D from the remaining piece of Fabric #1 according to the actual measurements of these sections, adding ½" to each dimension to allow for ¼"-wide seam allowances all around.

9. Mark a quilting design that does not reach all the way to the edges, to allow space for attaching the Prairie Points. (See design drawing on page 87.)

10. Cut backing and batting at least 1" larger than the quilt all around. Baste the 3 layers together; quilt.

11. Make and attach the Prairie Point edging to fit the edges of the quilt (2 lengths of 16 triangles and 2 lengths of 12), following the directions at right.

12. Lay the Prairie Points on top of the quilt, pointing them inward and adjusting them as needed so the points meet neatly at the 4 corners. Sew them to the quilt top and batting only, ¼" from the raw edge of the quilt top. Keep the backing free and folded out of the way.

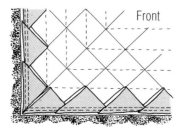

Backing folded out of the way.

13. Trim the batting only, as close to the machine stitching as possible. Open out the Prairie Points so the raw edges are turned under and baste. Turn under the raw edge of the backing to meet the machine stitching, trim if necessary, and baste. Slipstitch the backing in position so that it hides the machine stitching but can't be seen between the Prairie Points from the front. Remove the basting.

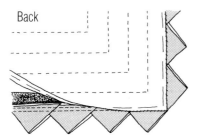

14. Embroider a label with the baby's name, date of birth, and any other relevant details, and sew it to the back of the quilt.

Prairie Points

To make Prairie Points, fold squares of fabric diagonally into quarters to make triangles. Insert each triangle a little way between the folds of the previous one and machine stitch them into a chain. Make 4 lengths that correspond to the quilt measurements.

Creative Variations

- To increase the dimensions of the quilt, enlarge the templates and the central panel. A template of 2½" from point to point (finished size) would increase the overall quilt measurements to 30" x 40". (See pages 141–42 for alternate templates of various sizes.)
- Shade the fabrics in the opposite direction, from dark in the center to light at the edges.
- Finish the edges in a different way. (See pages 127–33.)
- Use different fabric. The crib quilt shown at right was made from scraps of a wool/cotton blend, which would be warmer for a winter baby. The plain center panel was quilted in brightly colored pearl cottons to echo the patchwork shapes, and the edges were bound with a double binding.

Emmet's Quilt by Deirdre Amsden, 1992, London, England, 24" x 32". This quilt is a winter version made with assorted scraps of wool/cotton blend fabrics and thicker batting. The border provides design interest and the quilting in the center echoes the shapes of the patchwork.

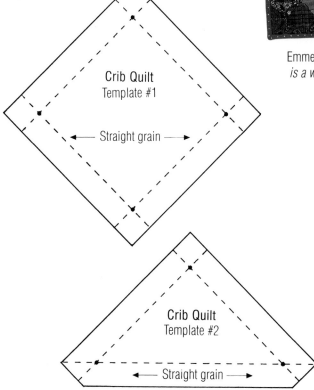

Crib Quilt
Template #1

← Straight grain →

Crib Quilt
Template #2

← Straight grain →

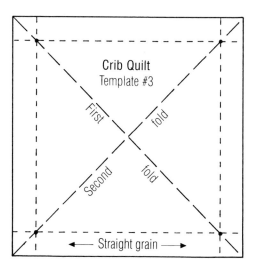

Crib Quilt
Template #3

First fold

Second fold

← Straight grain →

MINIATURE WALL HANGING: COLOURWASH FRAMED X

Colourwash Framed X *by Deirdre Amsden, 1991, London, England, 11" x 14". Collection of Mary F. Fortune. Photograph by Paul Seheult.*

Shaded design drawing showing suggestion for quilting (broken lines).

This miniature wall hanging suggests a garden viewed through a window. Like artists in other media, every quiltmaker has a preferred scale, and miniaturization is currently gaining recognition.

Skill Level: Intermediate

Dimensions: 11" x 14".

Template: #1 (page 93)

Materials

Assorted finely woven cotton prints in medium- to small-
scale designs*
⅓ yd. fabric (36" or 44" wide) for backing and binding
13" x 16" piece of low-loft batting
Sewing and fine quilting thread

*Pieces left over from larger projects or small swatches sent
out by mail-order companies are ideal. The hanging requires a total of 252 squares. To give yourself some choice,
you will need about 300 different prints. For such a small-
scale piece, it is probably best not to repeat prints.*

Preparation

1. Make Template #1. See below right.
2. Wash and press all your fabrics. This may already be
   done if they are scraps left over from other projects. I
   wash the tiny swatches from mail-order companies
   by dunking them in a bowl of very hot water. I fish
   them out with a fork onto a clean towel, pat out the
   surplus water, and finish drying them by pressing
   with an iron.
3. Mark and cut out at least 300 patches. Lay out your
   palette in 4 rows: dark, medium-dark, medium-
   light, and light. (See page 71.)

Construction

1. Arrange the patches, referring to the design drawing
   or one of the alternate designs below.

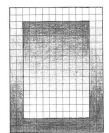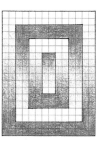

Alternate design layouts for miniature hanging.

2. Sew the patches together as described on pages 110–
   16. Be particularly careful to match seams accurately as you join the sections. Press the seams open
   except where you wish to add emphasis.
3. Mark the quilting pattern.
4. Layer and baste the top, batting, and backing together; quilt.
5. Finish with a narrow, single-layer binding (pages
   128–32). Cut the binding strips 1¼" wide. Add a
   narrow sleeve to the back if you wish to hang the
   completed quilt (pages 134–35).

Creative Variations

- Several of the designs in this book could be adapted
  to miniature patchwork. (See "The Four Seasons"
  on page 25, "Sunrise and Sunset" on page 144, and
  "Colourwash Framed VIII" on page 145.)

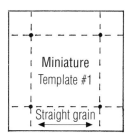

Miniature
Template #1

Straight grain

GROUP QUILT: SWEET PEA PINWHEEL

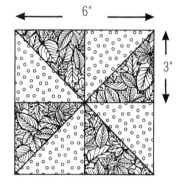

Sweet Pea Pinwheel *by members of The Marsh Quilters (illustration by Deirdre Amsden), 1990, London, England, 68" x 80" Collection of Ann Piper.*

Skill level: Intermediate

Dimensions: 68" x 80"

Template: #1, below

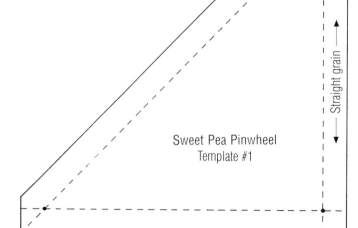

Sweet Pea Pinwheel
Template #1

The Colourwash principle is applied here to a group quilt called "Sweet Pea Pinwheel." The blocks as a whole, rather than the individual patches, are made up in a range of values and shaded together. The group chose a Pinwheel block for its simple shapes and counterchange arrangement. Instead of using highly contrasting values within each block, they used similar ones and shaded the blocks from dark to light diagonally across the quilt. They based their color scheme on the colors of the sweet pea flower: pinks, mauves, reds, purples, and greens. (The completed quilt was not available for photography.)

Materials

44"-wide fabric
Assorted fabric scraps from each participant's collection
1 yd. for borders
4 yds. for backing
½ yd. for binding
72" x 84" piece of batting
Sewing and quilting thread

Preparation

1. The block design, scale, and size of the finished quilt should be decided by the group. Take into account the number of people participating and the work load each person is willing to carry. The "Sweet Pea Pinwheel" quilt has a total of 120 blocks (10 across by 12 down).

2. Divide the number of blocks required by the number of participants. The diagonal shading of "Sweet Pea Pinwheel" requires approximately equal numbers of dark, medium, and light blocks. For maximum variety of fabrics, have each person make dark, medium, and light blocks. For example, if 20 people make a total of 120 blocks, each person will need to make 6 blocks (2 dark, 2 medium, and 2 light). Make a few spare blocks to give some choice when arranging the blocks. The leftover spares can always be made up into cushions.

    Each block, whether dark, medium, or light, requires 2 fabrics that are almost, but not quite, equal in value. The block design should be visible but not emphatically so.

3. Decide on the color scheme, based on the fabrics available to you (or to the group).

4. Distribute a set of clear instructions to include all the decisions made by the group, a scale drawing of the block, and a full-size drawing of the template. Advice on preparation of fabrics, method of construction, pressing instructions, number of blocks required, the reason for making the quilt, and a realistic deadline are also helpful.

Note

To ensure accuracy, it would be a good idea to provide group members with a template. If one person makes all the templates for the group, the blocks are more likely to turn out the same size, a decided plus when it's time to sew the blocks together.

Construction

1. Make Template #1. (page 94).
2. Cut the required number of Template #1 from your fabrics, referring to the design layout.
3. Assemble the required number of Pinwheel blocks, following the piecing diagram below.

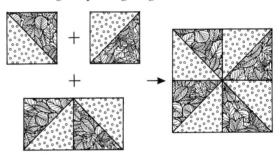

4. When all the blocks are complete, allot time and space for arranging them. When the blocks are laid out in their final arrangement, decide upon the border. Then devise a method of numbering the blocks so they can be assembled easily and without confusion. Add 4"-wide borders last.
5. Mark a quilting design or rely on the piecing as a guide to outline quilt the patchwork shapes.
6. Layer the quilt top with batting and backing; baste.
7. Quilt in a frame, with each participant taking their turn, or pass it around with a hoop so each person can quilt her own blocks.
8. Bind the edges.

Creative Variations

See page 40 for other block designs suitable for a group quilt, using a shaded arrangement.

Wall Hanging: Colourwash Stripes and Blue Triangles

Colourwash Stripes and Blue Triangles *by Deirdre Amsden,
1991, London, England, 64½" x 40½". The Colourwash
stripes provide a background for a shimmer of
brightly colored triangles. Exhibited in* Visions—The Art
of the Quilt, 1992–1994. *Photograph loaned by
Quilt San Diego, C & T Publications.*

Drawing showing shading suggestions for the Colourwash
stripes (repeat across to the right) and the blue triangles (repeat
on the left). Also a suggestion for meander quilting diagonally
from the center is indicated by broken lines.

This simple design of Colourwash stripes is overlaid
with brightly colored triangles, which are also shaded
from dark to light.

Skill Level: Intermediate/advanced

Dimensions: 64½" x 40½"

Templates #1, #2, #3, and #4 (page 98)

Materials

Small scraps of assorted print fabrics, enough for 640 squares*

A selection of brightly colored fabrics, ranging in value from dark to light for the triangles. You will need approximately ¾ yard total.

2 yds. for backing

½ yd. for binding

44" x 68" piece of batting

Sewing and quilting thread

Divide 640 by 4 values (dark, medium-dark, medium-light, and light) to get a minimum of 160 prints of each value. To give yourself choice, aim for at least 180–200 different fabrics in each value. (See "Extending Your Fabric Palette" on pages 61–63 and "Cutting to Make the Most of Prints" on page 71.)

Preparation

1. Make Templates #1, #2, and #3. (page 98).
2. Trace the checking template (#4) onto transparent template plastic and mark the position of the diagonal seam.
3. Wash and press all your fabrics.
4. Using Template #1, mark and cut squares for the Colourwash stripes.
5. Sort the squares into 4 value piles and lay out your palette of patches. (See page 71.)

Construction

1. Arrange the patches into stripes 2 squares wide x 20 squares long. Work from the 2 center stripes outward. Shade the stripes in opposite directions, using 5 pairs of darks, 5 pairs of medium-darks, 5 pairs of medium-lights, and 5 pairs of lights to make the transition from dark to light in each stripe. Refer to the design drawing.
2. Use Template #2 to mark and cut 272 bright triangles. Arrange the triangles over the correct

squares, following the design, or if you prefer, arrange the triangles in one of the following ways:

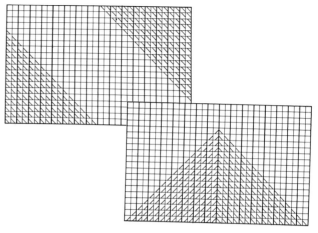

3. To sew the bright triangles in position, follow the 7 steps below.

   a. Pick up a few squares at a time with their triangles in position. Stack them in sequence, with the first to be picked up (A) at the bottom.

   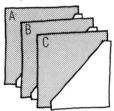

   b. Take them to your cutting board and use Template #2 to mark and trim off the correct corner on each square. If your template is made from durable material, you can use a rotary cutter to trim the corners. Stack the trimmed squares, with their triangles positioned ready for sewing. Square A should now be on top.

   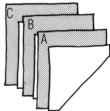

   c. Thread your sewing machine with a color that matches the bright triangles. Feed the squares and their triangles through the machine in sequence. Square A goes through the machine first.

   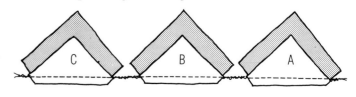

d. Cut the string of patches apart and stack them in sequence. Square A should be back on top.

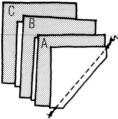

e. Press the seams open or to one side and restack them as you go. Square A should now be at the bottom.

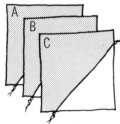

f. Use the checking template to make sure each square is still accurate. Mark and trim off any inaccuracies that may have occurred and stack the squares in sequence as you do so. Square A should once again be on top.

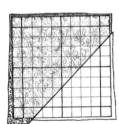 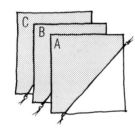

g. Replace the squares in the same order in which you picked them up.

4. When all the bright triangles have been sewn in place, use the Five-Step Sequence to sew the patches together. (See "Sewing Patches and Matching Seams" on pages 110–11 and "Colourwash Sewing Sequences" on pages 113–14.)
5. Give the patchwork a final press.
6. Layer the quilt top with batting and backing; baste.
7. Quilt diagonally from the center line outwards in meandering wavy lines as shown in the design drawing on page 96.
8. Finish the edges with a double-layer binding as shown on pages 128–32. Attach a hanging sleeve (pages 134–35) to the top edge, if desired.

Creative Variations

- The bright triangles could be arranged in any number of ways or omitted, leaving the striped design to stand on its own, perhaps as a vertical design.
- If you wish to design your own quilting pattern, mark it *before* basting the layers together.

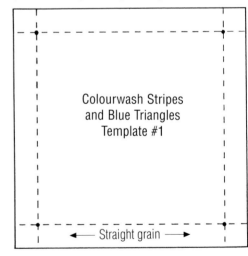

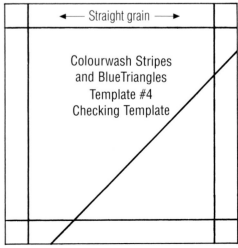

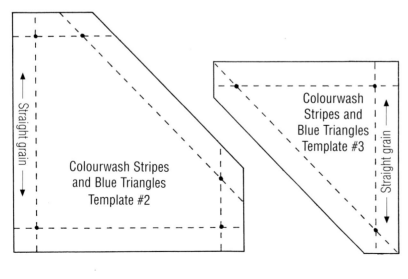

BED QUILT: LOG CABIN COLOURWASH

Log Cabin Colourwash *by Deirdre Amsden, 1990, London, England, 70" x 70". Machine pieced and hand quilted.*

This summer quilt consists of nine blocks with a pieced strip bordering the whole quilt. It was made without batting, using reversible Log Cabin blocks, in which the top and backing were pieced together, eliminating the need to quilt. However, the piecing must be extremely accurate so the "logs" on the front match the backing strips. Of course, you may assemble the required Log Cabin blocks, add batting and backing, and quilt traditionally if you prefer a heavier, warmer quilt and easier construction.

While a true Log Cabin quilt is made of strips sewn around a center square, in this design the "strips" are each pieced from squares. See step 1 under "Log Construction" on page 100.

The resulting quilt will fit a twin bed with an overhang of approximately 14" on each side. (It will not cover the pillows.)

Skill Level:
Advanced

Dimensions:
69" x 69"

Template: #1
(page 86)

3"

1½"

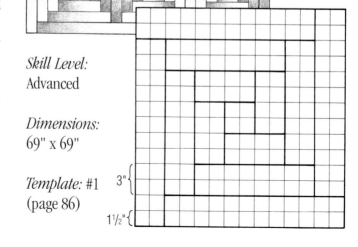

Materials

Assorted prints in dress-weight and lightweight cottons. The quilt is 46 x 46 squares for a total of 2,116. You will need to collect approximately 1,600 prints, about 400 each of 4 values (dark, medium-dark, medium-light, and light). If you cut 2 patches from at least half the fabrics, you will have a choice of about 2,400 patches, but you may need more. (See "Cutting to Make the Most of Prints" on page 70 and "Extending Your Fabric Palette" on pages 61–63.)

5 yds. of 44"-wide fabric for backing
8¼ yds. of piping cord
1 yd. fabric for bias strips to cover the piping cord
Sewing thread

Preparation

1. Make Template #1. See page 86.
2. Wash and press all your fabrics. (See "Fabric Preparation" on page 61.)
3. Mark and cut 2,400 patches, 600 from each of 4 values. Sort into 4 piles (dark, medium-dark, medium-light, and light) and lay out. (See page 71.)

Log Construction

You will need to make 5 blocks with light centers and 4 with dark centers.

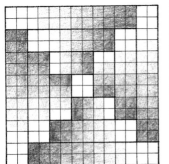

Make 5.

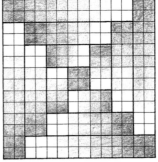

Make 4.

1. Arrange one block at a time, starting with the middle block, which has a light center. Pick out 4 light patches that blend together well and start to arrange the pieced "logs" around them, shading from dark to light as shown in the design drawing. The inner pieced logs are 4 squares long by 2 squares wide so you have to use 1 pair of each value as you shade from dark to light. The middle pieced logs are 8 squares long (2 pairs of each value), and the outer ones are 12 squares in length (3 pairs of each value). When the center of the block is light, the pieced logs shade from dark to light counterclockwise. When the center is dark, they shade from light to dark, also counterclockwise.

2. When you are satisfied with the arrangement, you can start piecing. However, take note that the blocks that surround this first one will need to relate to it to effect a smooth blend. You may wish to arrange some of the adjacent blocks before you begin sewing. Likewise, arrange the borders before piecing the edge blocks if at all possible.

3. Begin by piecing the 4 center patches, then piece all the logs. Take great care to be accurate. Do not sew the centers and pieced logs together yet.

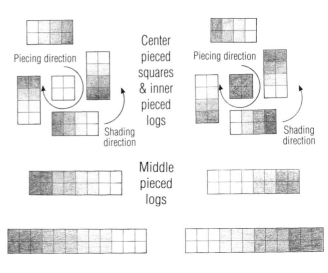

Outer pieced logs

4. Measure all completed pieced logs. First check the dimensions of the center square and the widths of each pieced log. They should all measure approximately 3½". No matter if they are slightly more or less, as long as they all measure the same. Make adjustments to your piecing if necessary and note the final measurement. Now note the lengthwise

measurements of each pieced log. The 4 inner ones should all measure the same (ideally 6½"). The middle and outer ones should ideally measure 12½" and 18½", respectively. Adjust the piecing so all the pieced logs in each group correspond. Try to get the pieced logs in each new block you piece to come out the same as these.

Cutting the Backing Strips

1. On the backing fabric, measure, mark, and cut with scissors (or rotary cutter) 43 strips, each 3½" wide (or the width of your pieced logs), marking or cutting across the fabric width (crosswise grain). Set aside 8 strips for the border.
2. From the remaining 3½"-wide backing strips, cut:
   36 outer strips, each 18½" long (or the length of your outer pieced logs)
   36 middle strips, each 12½" long (or the length of your inner pieced logs)
   9 center squares, each 3½" x 3½" (Cut from the leftovers after cutting the middle strips.)
   28 inner strips, each 6½" long (or the length of your inner pieced logs)
   From each of the 8 strips you set aside for the border, cut an inner strip 6½" long. You should now have a total of 36 inner strips.
3. Stack all the backing strips into piles by size.

Block Assembly

1. Place the pieced center square on top of a backing square, wrong sides together, and baste.

2. Mark the seam line on the wrong side of the first inner pieced log. Pin it to the center square, matching seams. Pin a corresponding backing strip in position on the underside so that the right sides of the log and strip are facing each other and the center

square is sandwiched in between. Sew half the seam only, through all 4 layers. Turn both the front pieced log and the backing strip right side out and press.

Sew a half-seam

3. Mark the seam line of the next inner pieced log. Pin to the center square and first log, matching seams. Pin the corresponding backing strip in place and stitch through all 4 layers.

4. Turn both the pieced log and the backing strip right side out and press. Sew the next 2 inner pieced logs and backing strips into position in the same manner. Finally, complete the first half seam.

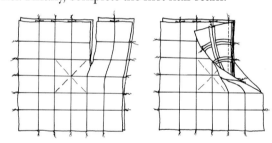

5. Sew the middle round of pieced logs and backing strips, following exactly the same procedure and direction (clockwise).
6. Sew the final round of outer pieced logs and backing strips in place, following the same instructions. *Do not snip off the threads at the outer edge of the block.* When you sew the blocks together, you will need to unpick some seams a little way and use the extra thread for resewing.
7. Make the remaining 8 blocks, following the steps above and referring to the block illustrations for value placement.

Joining the Blocks

1. Sew the blocks into 3 rows of 3 blocks each. First unpick the 2 seams marked by arrows in the diagram, gently pulling the stitches out without breaking the threads. Undo them ½" to release the top and backing from each other. Use the thread ends to resew the top sections together and the backings together.

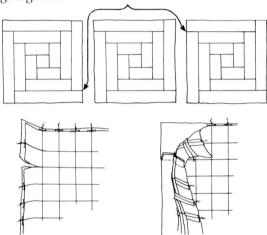

2. Join 2 edge blocks to a middle block to make a row. With right sides together, pin the right side of the edge block to the right side and backing of the center block, matching all seams. Stitch, keeping the edge block's backing strip free. Leave the thread ends uncut for the moment. Press the seams toward the edge blocks. Make the other 2 rows in the same manner.

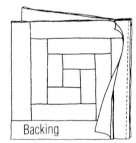

Backing

3. Neaten the back of the center row of blocks, but not the top and bottom rows. Turn the raw edge of the free backing strip under and pin in position to hide the machine stitching. Slipstitch in place.

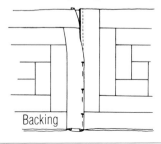

Backing

4. Now unpick the 3 seams indicated by arrows in each of the 2 top and bottom rows of blocks. Unpick them ½" as before to release the backing strips and resew fronts to fronts and backings to backings by hand, using a backstitch. You can now snip off all unneeded thread ends.

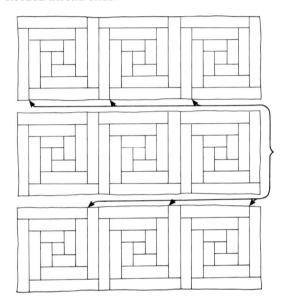

5. Join the rows of blocks together as described above, matching all seams and finishing the back by hand.

6. If you have not already arranged the patches for the border strips, do so now, paying careful attention to the design drawing on page 99 for value placement. You will need to piece 44 pairs of patches together for each border strip.

7. After piecing the patches together, check to make sure they match the dimensions of the completed quilt center and that they all measure the same. Adjust the seams if needed.

8. Using the 8 backing strips set aside, make border strips to match the length of the pieced border strips.

9. Sew the borders around the quilt in the same manner that you added the pieced logs and backing strips to the blocks. Pin carefully, matching every seam. Start the first seam 3" to 4" in from the edge, in the manner of a half seam so you can complete it once the final border has been added. Do not snip off the thread ends yet.

10. Before piping the edges, (page 103) unpick the 4 border seams for ½" to release the backing, resewing them by hand as before.

Piping

1. Preshrink piping cord by boiling it for 5 to 10 minutes. The cord may still draw up a bit after you wash the quilt. If you notice that happening, just tug it back into shape as it dries.

2. Cut a bias strip wide enough to encase the piping cord plus ½" for seam allowances. Join the strips with a diagonal seam as shown for bias-cut strips on page 129.

3. With the right side out, fold the bias strip over the cord. Baste ¼" from the raw edge to encase the cord.

4. Align the raw edges of the piping with the raw edge of the quilt top. Pin in place, keeping the backing free and out of the way. Clip the raw edge of the piping fabric at the corners to make it easier to position and stitch piping in place.

5. Using a zipper foot on your machine, stitch as close to the piping cord as possible without catching it. Leave approximately 4" unsewn at the beginning and end for the final join.

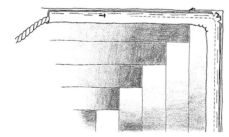

6. Unpin the 2 ends of the piping from the quilt. Remove any basting to free both the cord and the bias strip. Carefully measure and join the strip ends with a diagonal seam as shown for binding on page 131 (Step 12).

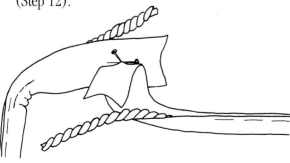

7. Splice the cord ends together to fit the gap exactly and bind with thread.

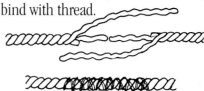

8. Encase the cord in the bias strip once again and baste. Pin in position and complete the stitching.

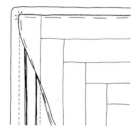

9. Turn in the raw edges of the backing so that the piping is along the outer edge of the quilt. Turn in the raw edge of the backing so that the folded edge hides the line of machine stitching. Baste and slipstitch into position.

Creative Variations

- To increase the overall size of the quilt, you can enlarge the size of the template. A 1¾" square would increase the quilt to 80½" x 80½" (and each log to 3½" wide). A 2" square would increase it to 92" x 92" (4" logs).

- An alternative block shading appears below in which all blocks have a dark center square. Instead of shading from dark to light, the logs either shade gradually from dark to medium-dark or from light to medium-light. This creates softer contrasts and dark diagonals across the quilt.

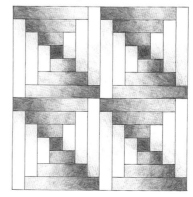

MOSAIC PATCHWORK

Mosaic Patchwork *(work in progress) by Deirdre Amsden, 1993, London, England. I based this repeat design on the pattern of cobblestones arranged in a clamshell design, one you often see in some Paris streets.*

On a recent visit to a Roman villa on the Isle of Wight, I was admiring its fine mosaic floors. It then occurred to me to use small scraps of fabric in a similar fashion. Geometric, appliqué, and pictorial shapes can all be freely adapted to mosaic. The tiny "tiles" make an attractive fragmented design requiring no exacting construction techniques.

Skill Level: All, but you should enjoy small-scale, fiddling work.

Templates: #1, #2, *or* #3 (page 105). Template #1 will give a "tile" measuring approximately ⅜" square; #2 will measure about ½" square; and #3, about ⅝" square.

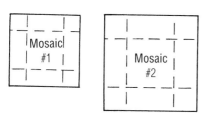

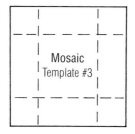

Use only one of these three templates depending on desired finished size.

Materials

Small scraps of finely woven print or plain fabrics in
several values
A firmly woven fabric for the foundation
Fine basting thread and assorted sewing threads to match
your fabric scraps

Preparation and Construction

1. Make Template #1, #2, *or* #3, above.
2. Cut the fabric patches by holding the template onto
the scrap of fabric and cutting around it with a small
pair of sharp scissors. The tiles do not need to be
absolutely precise.
3. Turn the raw edges in to meet each other in both
directions. Finger press and baste with a few stitches
to hold the turned edges in place. You will need to
remove this basting, so try not to use knots.

4. When you have prepared enough tiles, start arranging them into a design. One way to do this is to pin
the tiles onto a piece of light-colored pin-board
(Homosote) that will hold the pins fairly securely.
Short pins are ideal for this job. Stick a pin through
the center of each tile. Don't push the pins all the
way in or they will be difficult to remove.
5. When your design is pinned out, carefully transport
it to a photocopier. Protect the glass plate of the photocopier from the pinheads with a sheet of clear plastic, which the photocopy shop should be able to supply. If you find light creeping in because the pins
hold your design away from the glass plate, cover it
with sheets of paper to cut out the light.
6. The pinheads will show up as little white dots on the
copy. Prick each dot with a large tapestry needle.

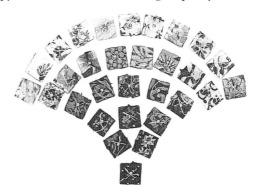

7. Lay the perforated photocopy onto your foundation
fabric, image side up. Pin it in position and mark
through the holes with a sharp contrasting-color
pencil. The position of each tile will now be marked
on your foundation fabric.
8. Transfer the tiles, one at a time, from the board to
your foundation fabric, using the marked dot as a
guide. Sew them in position with small slipstitches.
As you sew, use the point of the needle to poke under
any edges that stick out. Remove the basting.
9. Once the sewing is completed, you can frame the
mosaic as a picture, use it in a quilt, or use it to decorate any number of small items.

Night-time Blues *by Deirdre Amsden, 1987, London, England, 85" x 68 ½". This quilt was inspired by a memory of walking along a country road one clear, frosty winter night and seeing a sky full of stars. I wanted to convey the great, tranquil dome of the night sky as seen from the earth, yet hint at the fury of the universe we see in photographs of space. Collection of Helen Collis and Martin Hildyard. Photograph by John Coles.*

MAKING TEMPLATES

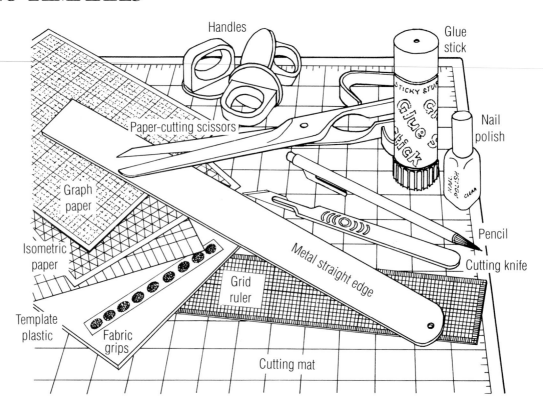

Since I prefer to cut each piece individually for my quilts, I use templates. If you prefer rotary cutting, you can cut squares of the appropriate size from strips, but you may need templates to cut other shapes.

I make templates out of model makers' high-impact polystyrene, a durable plastic that is not brittle and breaks cleanly when scored with a sharp knife. Template plastic is available in most quilt shops. Good-quality cardboard, at least ¹⁄₁₆" thick, is an acceptable alternative.

In addition to template plastic, gather the following supplies for template making:

Fabric grips (small dots of sandpaper with an adhesive backing) to keep templates from slipping
Clear nail polish or quick-drying varnish to coat the edges of cardboard templates for durability
Sharp cutting knife and replacement blades
Metal straight edge or acrylic quilters' ruler
Cutting mat with self-healing surface
Handles to affix to templates (optional). I use ones with strong adhesive pads that stick the handle firmly to the template. Handles with suction-cup bottoms that

can be transferred from one template to another are also available.

To make templates:
1. Draw basic shapes on graph or isometric paper and add a ¼"-wide seam allowance around each one.
2. Cut the shapes out, leaving an extra margin of paper all around. Glue the cutout to your template material and allow it to dry.
3. Place a metal cutting edge exactly on the line. Hold the knife blade upright against the cutting edge and cut out the templates. If you used cardboard, paint the edges with clear nail polish or quick-drying varnish to coat them and make them last longer.

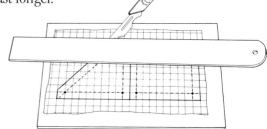

4. Attach a handle to templates large enough to accommodate them. Also apply fabric grips to each corner on the underside.

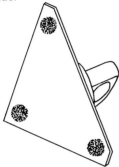

5. If there are pieces that require a set-in seam (page 112), pierce a hole at the intersection of the seams. This point is marked with a dot on all templates in this book. Make the hole large enough to mark through with a sharp pencil.

6. Using a permanent pen, label each template for easy identification. Include the design name, template number, and size (or the size of the block and cutting instructions, if relevant). As I use my templates over and over again for many different designs, I identify them by size only. It is not necessary to indicate the direction of the straight grain if you leave the graph paper stuck to your template. The lines will remind you how to place the templates correctly on your fabric. If you remove the graph paper, mark the direction of the straight grain on each template.

To cut the shapes from fabric:
1. Assemble the following:
   - Your prepared templates
   - Colored pencils (not watercolor pencils), including a silver one
   - Fabric eraser
   - Scissors for cutting fabric. I use lightweight patchwork scissors with a fine serrated blade which keeps fabric from slipping.

Because I use irregularly shaped fabric scraps, require different basic shapes for each quilt, and usually only cut a few shapes from each piece of fabric, scissors work best for me. If you prefer rotary cutting, by all means, cut the shapes you need from fabric strips of the appropriate widths. You will need a rotary cutter, mat, and acrylic ruler. I recommend Donna Lynn Thomas's book *Shortcuts: A Concise Guide to Rotary Cutting* as a basic reference.

2. Place your template on the right side of the fabric with the straight grain in the correct direction as indicated by the grain-line arrow and mark around it with a sharp pencil.

3. Cut the shapes from the fabric.

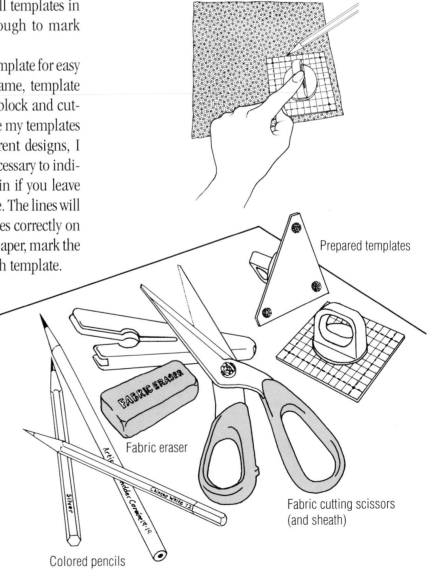

Prepared templates

Fabric eraser

Fabric cutting scissors (and sheath)

Colored pencils

SEWING THE PIECES TOGETHER

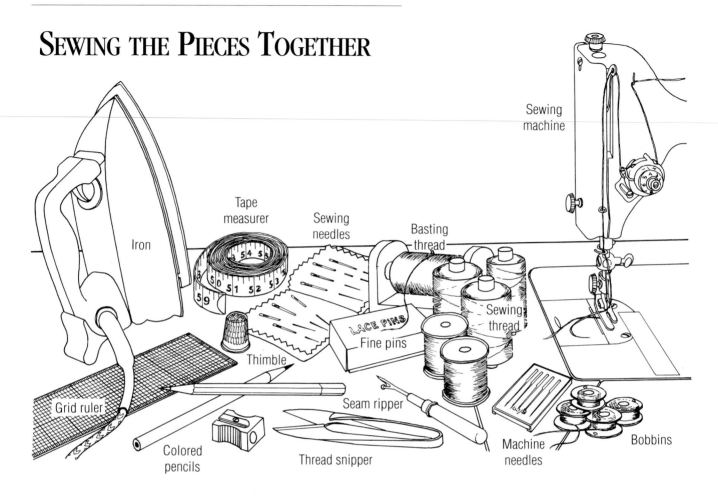

Machine Piecing

For the sake of clarity, I have divided the following explanation into two parts. The first deals with how to sew the patches together, and the second explains the sewing sequence. The quickest way to grasp both concepts is to make small practice samples as you read.

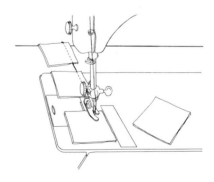

Sewing Patches and Matching Seams

1. Cut 16 squares, each 2" x 2".
2. Pick the patches up in pairs (eight), right sides together, and feed them through the machine one after another in a chain. Use the seam guide to maintain an accurate ¼"-wide seam allowance. Keep the machine running between the patches. The threads will twist into a fine chain.

3. Snip the threads and press seams open.
4. Put the pairs right sides together (four blocks of four). To mark the seam line on each top pair, align the 1¾" line on your grid ruler with the lower edge of the patches; mark lightly.

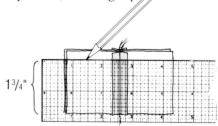

5. Line up the center seams and hold with a pin. Stitch.

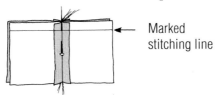

Marked stitching line

Bring the pin out on the marked line to match the seams securely at the point of seaming.

6. Next sew two blocks of four patches together (making two blocks of eight). Mark the seam line as before, this time measuring 1½" from the seam below instead of the edge. This seam line should cross the one you have just sewn.

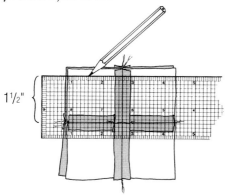

1½"

7. First align the two blocks by sticking a pin through the centers where the seams intersect. Now match and pin the two seams. Remove the pin at the center seam intersection. Stitch, using your hands to align the seams indicated by the arrows.

Measuring from the edge or seam below and aligning the intersecting seams ensure that the patches are sewn together accurately.

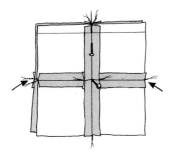

8. Sew one block of eight patches to the other eight-block unit. Mark the seam line, align all the intersections with pins, match and pin all the seams, and sew. Remember to align the seams indicated by arrows as you sew.

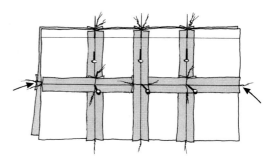

Matching and Sewing Diagonal Seams

1. Mark the seam line, using the points where two seams meet as a guide.
2. Use pins to align the seam intersections below the seam to be sewn. Then match and pin the seam intersections along the edge you are sewing.

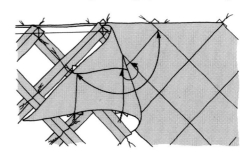

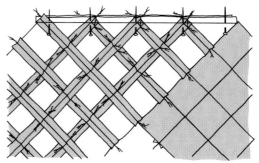

Set-in Seams

In the "Cubes" quilts on pages 77 and 137, I needed to use set-in seams from time to time. I mark the point of intersection for set-in seams with a dot through the holes in the template. See step 5 on page 109 under "Making Templates."

1. First draw the seam line between the marked dots (where the pins are in the illustration), using a grid ruler. Align the seam intersections below the seam to be sewn with a pin; match and pin the seams and the marked dots.

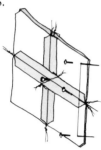

2. Sew the seam from dot to dot *only* (not beyond), using backstitching to lock the stitches at both ends.

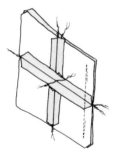

3. Sew the other seams, following the same procedure.

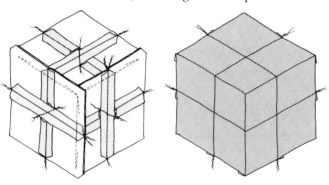

Half Seams

I use half seams to construct designs that do not easily break down into blocks or sections because there are no continuous seams, such as the "Cubes" quilts on page 77 and "Night-time Blues" on page 107. This is probably easier to explain using the following shapes:

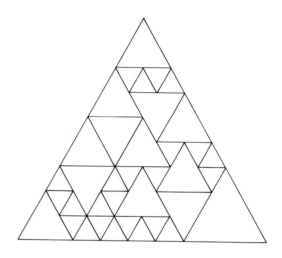

1. I first sewed as many triangles as I could into blocks: A, B, C, D, E, F, and G. I then joined A to B with a half seam.
2. This allowed me to sew C to AB, D to AC, and E to CD.
3. Then F was joined to D with a second half seam. This enabled me to complete the first half seam.
4. I sewed G to FB and then completed the second half seam.

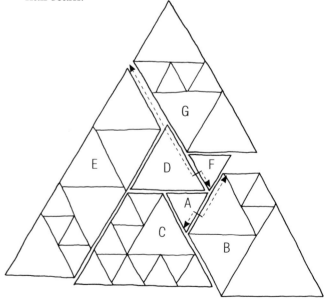

Colourwash Sewing Sequences

The following is the least confusing and most efficient sequence in which to sew patches together by machine. This method helps you keep all the patches in their rightful place and minimizes the number of times you have to stop and change to a new color of thread.

First decide upon a horizontal and a vertical direction, and which takes priority, for example:

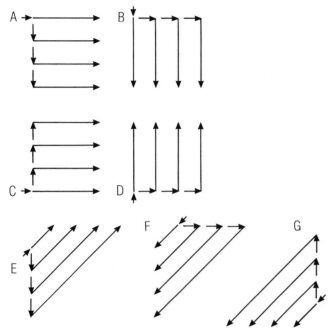

A. First move horizontally from left to right, then down to the next row, and so on.
B. First move vertically downward from top to bottom, then move to the left to the next row, and so on.
C. First move horizontally from left to right, then up to the next row, and so on.
D. First move vertically upward from bottom to top, then move to the left to the next row, and so on.
E, F, G. Diagonal variations.

I usually choose to work horizontally from left to right and then vertically from top to bottom. See sequence A in the illustration, above.

If you wish to practice along with the following directions, cut 20 patches, 2" x 2". Cut 8 light, 8 medium, and 4 dark, and arrange them as illustrated:

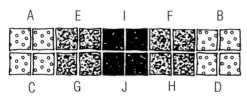

Five-Step Sequence

1. First thread your machine with light-colored thread. Now following sequence A, left, start at the top left-hand corner and move to the right along the top row, picking up the light-colored patches in pairs, placing them right sides together (pair A and pair B). Stack the pairs in sequence as you pick them up. Move to the next row down and pick up the light-colored patches, exactly as before, again moving from left to right (pair C and pair D). Stack them in sequence on top of the first pairs you picked up.

2. Feed the patches through the machine in a chain. The last pair to be picked up (pair D) is on top of the stack and will be sewn first. Use the seam guide to keep the ¼" seam accurate.

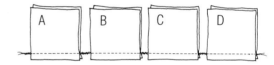

3. Snip the chain of patches apart, stacking them as you go. The last pair to go through the machine and the closest to you when you finish sewing (pair A) will be at the bottom of the stack once again.

4. Press the seams open, stacking the pairs in sequence as you do so. The first pair to be pressed (pair D) will now be at the bottom of the stack, and pair A will be on top ready to be replaced first.

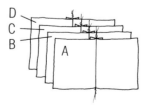

5. Replace the sewn patches in the empty spaces, starting at the top left-hand corner and moving to the right along the top row (pair A and pair B). Move to the next row down and replace the remaining pairs.

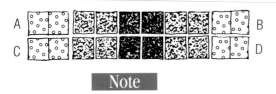

Note

As long as there are an odd number of steps in a sequence, the patches will go back in the order you picked them up.

Following the same five-step sequence, you can now sew the pairs into blocks of four. Mark the seam line as you pick up each pair. First pick up pair A and pair C by flipping pair A down over pair C so that their right sides are together. Mark the seam line along the top edge. Next, move to the right and pick up pair B and pair D in exactly the same way. Mark the seam line and stack on top of AC. Match and pin the seams and sew. Follow steps 2–5 until the blocks of four are once again back in position.

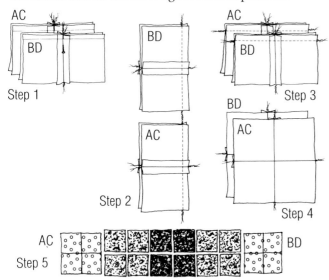

Next change the thread in the machine to a medium value and sew the medium-colored patches together. Pick up pair E first. Move to the right and pick up pair F next, then move down one row, picking up pair G and then pair H.

After sewing the medium-colored patches into blocks of four and replacing them, and before changing to dark

thread, sew the medium blocks to the light blocks. Pick up AC/EG first, then move to the right and pick up FH/BD. Follow the five-step sequence exactly.

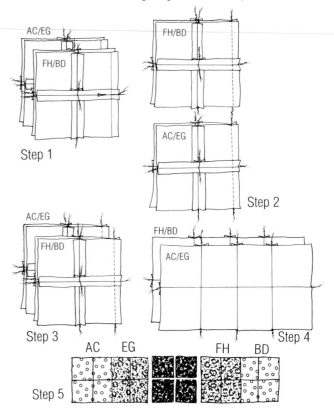

Finally, thread the machine with dark thread and sew pair I together and pair J together, then sew these two pairs into a block of four (IJ). Join IJ first to ACEG and then to FHBD.

Hand Piecing

Hand piecing is not much different from machine piecing. The same template and marking methods work. I backstitch seams that will be pressed open. You do not need to work in a strict sequence when hand piecing because you can replace patches before picking up the next ones. I suggest, however, that you still sew in an orderly fashion, and that you sew patches into pairs and pairs into fours, and so on.

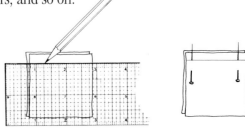

Blues in the Night *by Deirdre Amsden, 1991, London, England, 60" x 48½". A postcard of* Night-time Blues *(page 107) brought about this commission. It was hand pieced using the whipped method (below) and hand quilted. Collection of Laura Fisher. Photograph by the author.*

Whipped Piecing

Whipped piecing is a precise method of sewing patches together. It is particularly good for sewing geometric shapes that are difficult to seam together by machine, such as hexagons. This is how I pieced "Blues in the Night." I use freezer paper as the foundation for each piece and the method shown here.

1. Make a template the exact size of the finished patch, without seam allowances. See "Making Templates" on pages 108–109.

Template for whipped piecing used for cutting the paper shapes.

2. Place the template on the plastic-coated side of the freezer paper. Hold it firmly in position and cut out the shape, hugging the edge of the template with the scissors. *Cut a paper for each patch you need.*

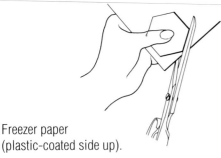

Freezer paper
(plastic-coated side up).

3. Place the papers, plastic-coated side down, onto the wrong side of the fabric, leaving at least ½" allowance between shapes. Align the shapes with the straight grain of the fabric, following your design. Press the paper in position and cut out with a ¼"-wide allowance on each edge.

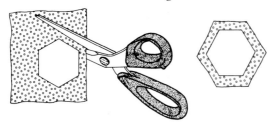

Iron freezer paper shape to *wrong* side of fabric.

4. Fold the raw edge of the fabric over the paper and baste through the paper and both layers of fabric. Do not knot the thread at the beginning and do not backstitch at the end. Instead, overlap the first stitch with the last stitch so it will be easy to remove the basting stitches later.

5. Hold the prepared shapes right sides together and whip them together from the wrong side, using small stitches and matching thread. Try not to sew through the paper and catch only a few threads of each folded edge with each stitch. Lock your seams by sewing backwards and forwards a few stitches.

6. Stitch through corners twice as an extra precaution.

Whipstitch folded edges together.

7. On reaching the edges, remove the basting to free the seam allowance along the edge before whipping the patches together. This will enable you to finish your quilt in any way you choose. (See "Finishing the Edges" on page 127.)

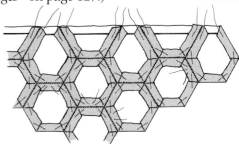

8. Remove the basting; press the patchwork with the papers left in position. Remove the papers carefully.

Pressing

Pressing is important for accuracy and for a flat, neat appearance. However, heat stresses fabrics, so keep it to a minimum without compromising good results.

1. Set the iron to suit your fabric's fiber content. Use a moderate setting for an assortment of fabrics. Be careful when ironing synthetic fabrics.
2. Finger-press seams first and then press down with the iron. Moving the iron back and forth over the patches can drag and distort them.
3. Press seams open in areas where you need the patches to blend together.
4. Press seams to one side only where you plan to emphasize a seam by quilting against it.
5. To press part of a seam to one side and the rest to the other side, first finger-press the seam open at the point of directional change, then ease the seams into the desired directions and press.

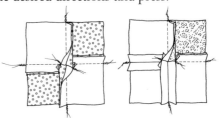

6. To press a dark fabric toward a lighter one, trim back the seam allowance of the dark one.

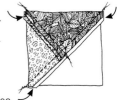

Trim the darker seam allowances.

ADDING THE BORDERS

If you are able to add your pieced borders, section by section, while you are constructing the central design, then you will have few problems making the borders fit correctly. However, if it is necessary to add borders in pieced strips, it is critical to measure the quilt carefully to determine the correct border lengths before attaching them. Anything other than an exact fit will result in the edges of your quilt being too tight or too loose, and it will not be square or hang correctly.

1. Measure the edges of your completed patchwork and across the center in both directions. If the edge measurements differ by more than 1" or 2" from the center one, it is wise to make some adjustments to your piecing along the edges to bring the three measurements into line. Base your final two border measurements on an average of the three vertical and three horizontal measurements, leaning toward the center measurements.

2. Measure your pieced borders and make any piecing adjustments necessary to make them correspond to your final quilt measurements exactly (step 1).

3. Draw seam lines on the borders, using a grid ruler.

4. Pin the two longest borders in place first, matching all seams and stitch. Press.

5. Attach the two shorter borders in the same way.

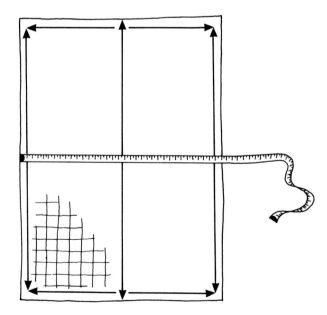

QUILTING

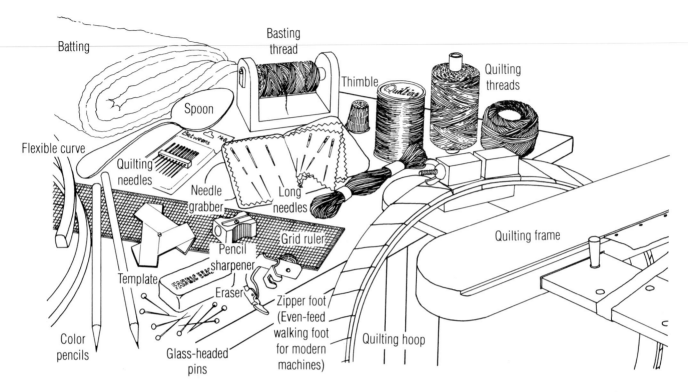

Plenty of commercially manufactured quilting templates are available these days, so you may be able to find designs of the right size. I make my own because I relate the quilting to the scale of the patchwork shapes. (See "Planning the Quilting" on pages 43–47.) I make them exactly the same way I make piecing templates, omitting the seam allowance. I draw or draft my shapes on graph or isometric paper, using a flexible curve to draw curved shapes. I then paste them onto my template material and cut them out. I also attach a handle if I can.

It is also possible to use the flexible curve like a ruler and eliminate the need for making a template. Establish your required curve, using the pieced shapes of your actual patchwork as a guide. Check that it works correctly on other areas of your patchwork and adjust the flexible curve if necessary before starting to mark.

Colourwash Diamonds. *Detail shows the quilting snaking across the quilt. This quilt is made from a wool/cotton blend twill weave. Photograph by John Coles.*

Colourwash Diamonds *by Deirdre Amsden, 1987, London, England, 50½" x 51½".*
"Diamonds" in the title refers to the shape of the template (a 60° diamond with 1¾" sides).
The idea for this quilt came from the traditional quilt pattern Thousand Pyramids.
Collection of Mr. and Mrs. Schwarz. Photograph by John Coles.

Marking

I use pencils that either match my quilting thread or blend with the colors in my quilt. I personally do not like using water-soluble pencils or pens, but you may swear by them. Always test new methods. The ideal marker remains visible while quilting and disappears once the quilting is completed, a real feat.

Before marking the quilting design, give the wrong side of the patchwork a final press. Then lay it out on a smooth, hard surface.

Mark systematically, evenly, and only as heavily as required to see the lines.

Basting the Layers

1. Make both the backing and batting larger than the quilt top by at least 2" all round.
2. Before laying out the backing, give it a final press. Fold it carefully into quarters without creasing and put a pin at the midpoint of each side.
3. Unfold the backing and lay it out wrong side up. Smooth out any wrinkles and tape the four corners to the floor or work table.
4. Fold the batting into quarters. Place it in one corner of the backing, using the marker pins as a guide. Unfold it carefully and gently smooth out any wrinkles, working from the center out to the edges.
5. Now fold your quilt top into quarters with the wrong sides out. Position it on one corner of the batting, using the marker pins as a guide once again. Unfold it carefully and gently smooth out any wrinkles, again working from the center out.

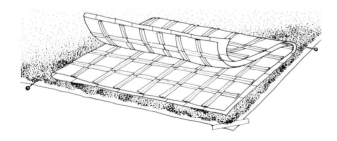

Place quilt top folded in quarters in one corner
on top of the batting/backing layers.

6. Pin the layers together at intervals (about 6"–12", depending on the size of your quilt). Work from the center out to the four sides and corners. This will hold the layers while you baste. If you prefer to pin-baste, you will need to pin more closely and may prefer safety pins.
7. Use white basting cotton, as there is a danger of unsightly dye spots being left by dark threads. If the quilt is dark colored, then a dark-colored basting cotton may be best.

To avoid knots, baste all the way across the quilt with one piece of thread. Unreel enough thread for half the distance without cutting it from the spool. Start in the center and baste in one direction. When you reach the edge, backstitch a few times; cut thread. Now wind off enough thread to baste to the opposite edge, cut, and starting in the center, baste to the edge.

Baste first from the center to the four corners, then from the center out to the four sides. Then baste in a grid (approximately 4" wide) across the rest of the quilt, still working from the midline out with one length of thread. Baste around the edges last. Make sure you baste to one side of any marked quilting lines.

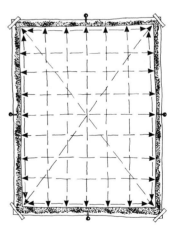

Baste the layers together.

A tip from a student many years ago, which I have found useful, is to baste against the edge of a spoon. This helps to guide the needle back up to the surface, and the bowl of the spoon lets you grasp the needle. I also keep basting thread in a spool holder that allows it to run freely.

Using a Hoop

A hoop has several advantages over a frame. It is portable, versatile, and space saving, and it can be rotated to ensure a comfortable quilting position most of the time. A quilt of any size may be quilted in a hoop.

Work in good light; daylight (but not bright sunlight) is best. Otherwise, use a lamp you can direct onto your work.

1. Plan to start quilting in the center if possible. Place the inner hoop flat on a table and center the quilt over it, marked side up. Unscrew the outer hoop a little to enlarge it and press it down over the quilt and the inner hoop. I weight the center of the quilt with a book to prevent the tension from becoming too taut as I press the outer hoop down.

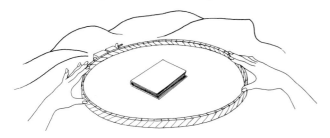

2. As you quilt, move the hoop outwards in ever-widening circles until you reach the edges. At this point, you will either need to change to a border hoop or baste a strip of fabric along the edges to accommodate your hoop.

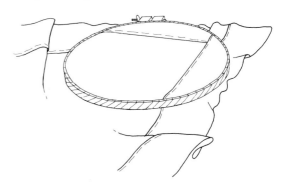

Baste strips of fabric to the outer edges of the quilt top to accommodate the hoop.

Take the quilt out of the hoop when you finish quilting for the day. If it remains in one position too long, there is a danger the hoop will permanently dent or flatten the batting.

Using a Frame

A frame holds the layers of a quilt firmly together. The following method requires no basting and is traditional to North Country and Welsh quilters in Britain. They quilt from one side of the quilt to the opposite side instead of from the center outwards.

My frame is simple. It rests on chairbacks and consists of two rails and two stretchers. The stretchers slip through slots in the rails, and pegs hold the rails apart the appropriate distance. See the illustrations on page 122.

1. Mark the center points of the webbing on the two rails. Fold the backing in half horizontally and mark the center point of each side with a pin. With the wrong side up, match the center points on the webbing to the center points of the backing and pin. Working from the center out, pin the backing to the two rails.

2. Neatly roll the backing around the far rail until the rails are about 30" apart. Slot and peg (or clamp) the stretchers in position so the backing is stretched but not taut.

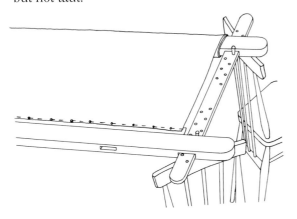

3. Lay the batting on the backing so that one edge is aligned with the near edge of the backing. Smooth it out gently and let it hang over the far rail.

4. Now lay the quilt top on the batting, right side up. Set it a short distance in from the edge and by eye, match the center point of the quilt top to the center point on the webbing. Make sure the edge of the quilt top is straight and parallel to the webbing. Pin. Then baste securely through all three layers.

5. Gently smooth out the quilt top, making sure it is straight and letting it hang over the far rail. Pin through all three layers at intervals along the far rail to keep the top and batting in place.

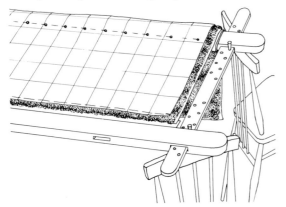

6. If the extra batting and the quilt top reach the floor, fold them up to the frame and hold them in position with pins. Cover with a clean sheet, which you can also use to cover the whole frame once quilting is finished for the day. (Cats assume a quilt in a frame is a padded hammock, and family members sometimes treat it as an extra table.)

7. Attach the sides of the quilt to the stretcher with cloth tape as shown, pinning through all three layers to prevent them waffling about while you are quilting.

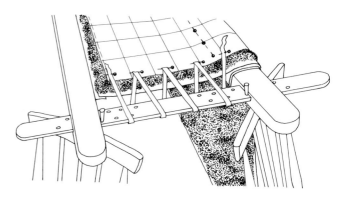

8. Start quilting near the center and work out toward the taped ends.

9. When you have quilted the first section, unpin the tapes. Unpeg (or unclamp) the stretchers and roll the quilted portion around the near rail. Unroll another portion of the backing from the far rail and remove all the pins that were holding the three layers together. Repeg (or reclamp) the stretchers in position with the same tension as before. Smooth out the batting and the quilt top, checking to see if everything is still straight and square, and repin along the far rail. Retape the ends and continue to quilt.

Hand Quilting

Hand quilting is an evenly spaced running stitch. Everyone's stitch size, spacing, and tension varies, but the evenness of the stitching is what makes quilting look its best. Fabric, batting, thread, and needle size also affect the look of hand quilting.

There is no "right" method. Some people rock the needle and some stab. Some take one stitch at a time; others take several. You have to find your own way and do whatever works for you. Several methods are described below. If one doesn't work for you after a fair try, move on to the next one. If you just cannot find a way and you do not enjoy quilting, then collaborate with someone who does. Quilting is not a penance.

Rocking Method

In this method, the sewing hand wearing the thimble controls the needle from the top. The hand underneath feels for the needle point as it emerges from the quilt layers. Then both hands, working in cooperation, guide the needle back up to the top again. By rocking the needle in and out, several stitches may be taken onto the needle before it is pulled through.

If you can't rock the needle in and out, or if it flies out of control as you are trying to bring it back up, it probably means your quilt is too taut. Try slackening it bit by bit until you can control your needle and the stitching.

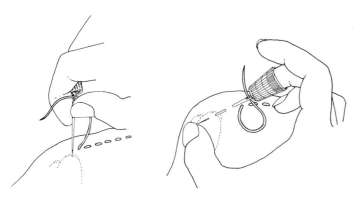

Begin each run of stitches with your needle held in a vertical position. With each "rock" of the needle, try to push it into the quilt as vertically as possible. (A tightly stretched quilt will not allow you this flexibility.) Stitch size (and space) is governed by how far you allow the needle to emerge on top (and below) before rocking it once again.

Two-Thimble Method

This method, devised by Michael James, protects the finger underneath the quilt with a second thimble. This thimble should have a defined ridge, which can be seen clearly as it is pushed up hard against the quilt layers from below. The quilt needs to be stretched at a tighter tension than for the rocking method. Take one stitch at a time across the thimble ridge. You can be sure the needle has passed through all the layers when you feel it glance off the metal ridge.

It is easy to produce small stitches using this method, and with practice, you can build up speed and rhythm even though you only take one stitch at a time.

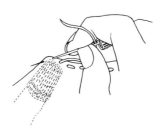

Stab-Stitch Method

I would not choose this quilting method, but many people prefer it. I do find it useful in awkward or bulky places, such as seam intersections.

Place one hand underneath the quilt. This hand will have to work by feel. Push the needle vertically down through the quilt layers. Pull the thread a little way through with the hand underneath and stab the needle back up vertically. Pull the thread all the way through with the top hand, feeling from underneath to make sure the thread does not tangle and knot on the back.

This stitching method produces closely spaced, small stitches on the top but less controlled ones on the back.

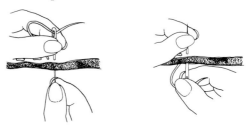

Place your sewing hand under the work.
Reverse the hand positions if you are left-handed.

These methods of quilting all take practice. The more you do, the better you become. If you leave off quilting for any length of time, it takes a while to get back into the rhythm. The first few stitches are always unnerving.

Locking the Stitches

1. To begin, insert the needle into the batting one needle-length from the start, along the line you are about to quilt. Bring it out at the start, leaving a tail of thread.
2. Take a small backstitch through the top and batting only. Then be quite certain to pierce this stitch with the point of the needle when taking the first stitch.

3. Continue quilting. Once past the tail of thread, either snip it off or run it off into the batting.

The thread is anchored by the split backstitch and also by the first few quilting stitches running over the thread lodged in the batting.

4. To stop, take a small reverse stitch through the top and batting only.

5. Pierce this stitch with the needle point as you run the thread through the batting along a line yet to be quilted. Bring the needle out, leaving a tail of thread. Once you have quilted past the tail, cut it or run it off into the batting.

6. If there is no convenient line along which to run the thread, then run it back alongside the last few quilting stitches. Bring the needle out as close to a stitch as possible.

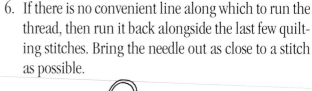

7. Slip the needle under the stitch and run it back, into the batting, along the other side of the quilting stitches. Cut the thread or run it off into the batting.

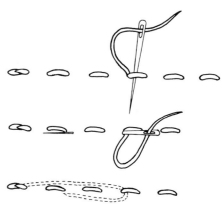

Occasionally, you can bypass locking your stitches. Whenever possible, use one thread to quilt in two directions as described in the basting method on page 120.

Only run the thread through the batting to the start of another line if it is less than a needle's length away and the thread is paler than the fabric. Anchor the first stitch of the new line by taking it in a backward direction.

Stitch Variations

There is no rule that says quilting must be a running stitch. Why not experiment with various stitches? You may also need to experiment with threads to make the following suggestions work to the best advantage.

- Sashiko quilting uses a thicker thread and a longer stitch with a short space between stitches.

- Try backstitching when the appearance of the back is unimportant.

- Do whipped quilting after you have completed a line of quilting by whipping a thicker second thread (matching or contrasting in color) through the quilting stitches with a rounded tapestry needle. See the photographic detail on page 79.

- To use an embroidery stitch, be sure to use a low-loft batting. Then try stitches, such as the chain stitch or herringbone stitch.

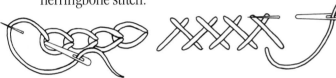

Chain stitch   Herringbone

- Try stipple quilting. Take stitches one at a time in a higgledy-piggledy fashion. See the photographic detail on page 79.

- Meander quilting wanders around the surface in wavy lines. See the photographic detail on page 79.

Suggestions for meander quilting

7. Appliqué ribbons, lace, or motifs with quilting stitches.

8. Thread a bead(s) onto the needle before taking a stitch to add sparkle and texture.

Machine Quilting

Many modern machines can be programmed to do decorative stitching or allover meander quilting. A good modern or industrial sewing machine is most suited to machine quilting; however, it is possible to quilt on an older machine with a few minor adjustments:

- Lessen the pressure of the presser foot.
- Set stitch length to 8–10 stitches per inch.
- Adjust the tension so the bobbin thread does not appear on the top but still looks right on the back.
- Change to an even-feed (walking) foot or use a quilting or zipper foot.
- Use a stronger needle: size #12 (80) or #14 (90).

A dense, low-loft batting is easier to machine quilt than a soft, springy one. There are several ways of basting the layers together in preparation for quilting:

To baste the layers for machine quilting:
- Baste in the regular way as described on page 120 or pin-baste, using either glass-headed pins or safety pins. Place pins parallel to the direction in which you intend to roll the quilt, with the pinheads toward you so they are easy to remove as you quilt.
- As extra insurance against shifting, baste the backing and batting together first and then baste the top in position.

I used the following method (described to me by fellow quilter Dieuwke Philpott) to quilt "Colourwash Stripe III" on page 126.

1. Baste the quilt top and batting together first and quilt all the lines that run with the straight grain in the quilt top.

2. Remove the first basting and then baste the backing in position.

3. Now quilt the lines that are on the bias. (This lessens the likelihood of puckers forming where lines of quilting cross. More interestingly, it also creates two depths of quilting. See the photo detail on page 79.)

Note

I have used nylon monofilament thread with a cotton/polyester bobbin thread on the few Colourwash quilts I have machine quilted. The transparent nylon thread takes on whichever color it crosses, but it is difficult to use. I recommend experimenting with machine embroidery and sewing threads, the finer quilting threads, or even metallic thread instead of the nylon monofilament thread.

If you use a zipper or quilting foot, be sure to quilt each line in the same direction (not first in one direction and then back in the other).

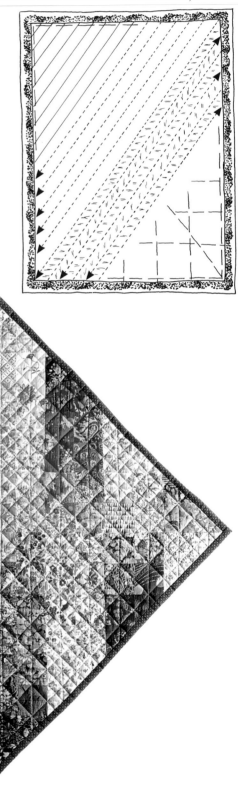

Colourwash Stripe III by Deirdre Amsden, 1986, Cambridge, England, 31" x 31" (point to point). Machine quilted with nylon monofilament thread. Collection of Clare Drummond. Photograph by Jacky Philips.

FINISHING THE EDGES

There are several ways to finish the edges of your quilt. The most common method is binding with a double or single layer of fabric. Directions for these two types of binding follow. Another that deserves mention is self-binding. This involves bringing the backing forward over the front of the quilt. Of course, you must allow an extra margin of backing for this purpose when you layer your quilt top with the batting and prepared backing. You will need at least twice the finished width of the binding, plus ¼" to turn under, plus a bit for insurance.

Self-Binding

To self-bind the edges:

1. Remove the basting around the quilt edge. Carefully trim the batting to the proposed width of your binding. Remember that the ¼"-wide seam allowance around the quilt top will be part of the binding. For example, if the binding is to be ¼" wide, trim the batting flush with the raw edge of the quilt top. If it is to be 1" wide, trim the batting ¾" from the edge of the quilt. Whether you use scissors or a rotary cutter, *take care to keep the backing out of the way while you trim the batting*.

2. Using a grid ruler, mark a cutting line on the backing. Measure twice the width of the binding from the raw edge of the quilt top. (For a ¼"-wide finished binding, measure ½". For a 1"-wide finished binding, measure 2".) Trim the backing along this line.

3. Turn the edges of the backing under ¼" and baste.

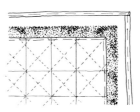

4. Bring the backing over the batting to the front, lapping ¼" over the raw edge of the quilt top. Fold the corners straight or into a miter. Pin and baste.

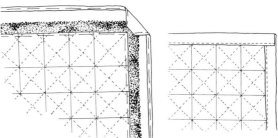

5. Slipstitch the binding in place or topstitch, either by hand or machine, through all the layers. If you wish, you can insert a piping or an edging, such as Prairie Points (page 90), under the binding before topstitching it down.

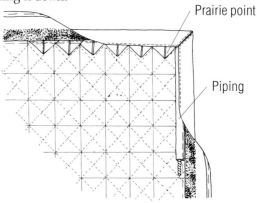

Prairie point

Piping

Single- and Double-Layer Binding

Whether you decide upon single- or double-layer binding, the first task is to prepare the quilt in the following manner.

Preparing the Quilt

1. Smooth out the quilt on your work table. Remove all basting except around the edges. Check the edge basting and rebaste any areas that have worked loose or snapped.
2. Measure the edges and across the center in both directions. Make a note of the six measurements. If all three vertical (and horizontal) measurements are equal, give yourself a pat on the back. More likely the three will differ slightly. A difference of 1" or so can be accommodated. More than that will mean adjusting the quilting. If the edge measurements are greater than the center one (which is most likely), then do more quilting in the border area. If the edges are tighter, you may have to consider removing some quilting in the border or doing more in the center.
3. Take the averages of your three vertical and three horizontal measurements, leaning toward the center measurements, and make a note of them.

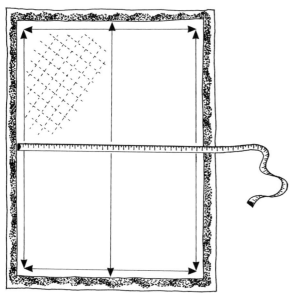

4. While the quilt is flat, check the squareness of the corners with a set square or right-angled triangle, and the straightness of the edges with a ruler. Mark irregularities with a colored pencil or trim the surplus batting and backing with a rotary cutter. Remember to take into account the width of your binding.

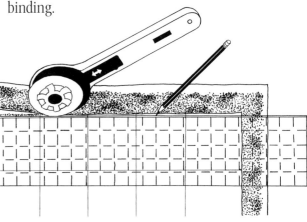

Cutting and Attaching Single- and Double-Layer Binding

Double binding is harder wearing and bulkier than single binding. Choose whichever method is suitable for the intended use and appearance of your quilt. Cut binding on the crosswise grain of the fabric. Bias binding is only essential for quilts with curved edges.

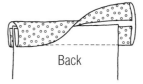

Back

Single-layer binding

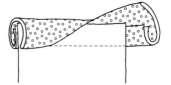

Double-layer binding

For single-layer binding: Cut strips four times the desired finished width of the binding, plus approximately ¼" (a little more if you are using a high-loft batting).

Note

A binding gadget, called a bias-tape maker, is useful for preparing single bindings whose folded-in edges meet in the center. Feed the binding into the wide end. Pull the gadget steadily by the handle, following it closely with the iron.

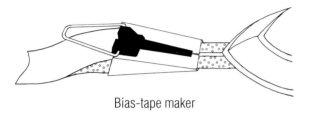

Bias-tape maker

For double-layer binding: Cut double binding six times the finished width of the binding, plus an extra ⅜"–½" to accommodate the thickness of the batting and fabric layers. Fold the binding in half lengthwise, wrong sides together, and press.

Note

You may need to cut several binding strips to make a piece long enough for the quilt top. Use a diagonal seam and press it open to distribute the bulk. Mitered corners (pages 130–31) require a continuous binding, so you need to make up a strip that reaches all the way around the quilt, plus an extra 8"–10" for the mitered corners and ease of handling. With this much extra, you won't run short.

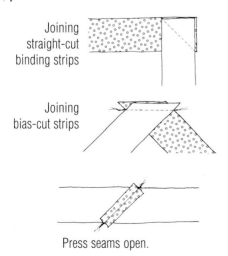

Joining straight-cut binding strips

Joining bias-cut strips

Press seams open.

In the directions below, straight corners are shown with single-layer binding and mitered corners with double-layer binding, but you may attach either type of binding with your choice of straight or mitered corners. Substitute the appropriate steps.

To attach single-layer binding with straight corners: Bind each side of the quilt separately. Bind the two longest edges first, unless you chose to add the top and bottom borders before the sides. The binding application should match the border application.

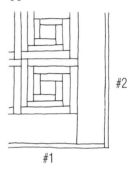

#2

#1

1. Cut and prepare two lengths of binding (based on the average measurement). Fold them in half crosswise and mark the center point of each with a pin.
2. Open out one folded-in edge on the binding strip. With right sides together, match the center point of the binding to the center point of the quilt edge, align the raw edges, and pin. Now pin the two ends of the binding in place. Pin the remainder of the binding in place, easing as necessary. Baste but do not remove pins.

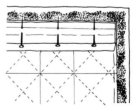

3. Machine stitch the binding in position along the crease. Remove the pins as you sew. Backstitch at both ends.

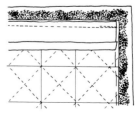

Backstitch

4. Remove all basting. Use a rotary cutter or scissors to trim the batting and backing to the width of your binding if you have not already done so. Turn the binding over to the back so the folded edge hides the machine stitching. Pin and slipstitch the binding in place.

5. Now cut and prepare binding for the two remaining sides, using your average measurement plus 2". Again mark the center points and match them to the center points of the top. Now pin the two ends in position, leaving an extra 1" hanging free at each end. Pin the remainder of the binding in position, baste, and stitch as before.

6. Fold up the binding and wrap the extra 1" around the ends. Then fold the binding over to the back and slipstitch in place.

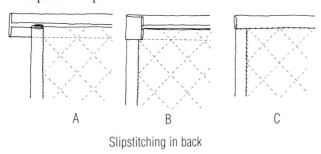

Slipstitching in back

To attach double-layer binding with mitered corners:

1. Prepare the binding by stitching strips together as shown above to make one long piece that will reach all the way around the quilt.

2. Fold the strip in half lengthwise with wrong sides together and press.

3. Start pinning the prepared binding strip to the edge that is closest to your average measurement. Leave approximately 4" of binding free to make the final join. Align the raw edges of the binding to the raw edges of the quilt top and start to pin. After a few pins, run the binding around the quilt edge to check that no binding seams fall at corners, which would spoil the miter. In the event that one does, readjust your starting position. Quickly recheck the corners and continue to pin until you reach the first corner.

4. Fold the binding up from the corner to make a 45° angle. Pinch the fold to crease it and open. Now put the last pin in along the diagonal crease. Measure along the edge to check that it corresponds to your average measurement and that you have not pulled the binding too tight during the pinning. Adjust if necessary. Baste but do not remove pins.

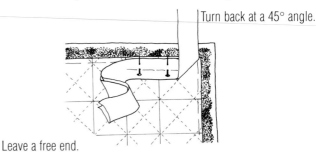

Turn back at a 45° angle.

Leave a free end.

5. Stitch the binding in position, using a ¼"-wide seam allowance. Sew right up to the diagonal crease and backstitch to lock.

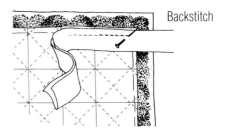

Backstitch

6. Refold the binding up along the original crease and back down over itself so it lies along the next edge.

7. Start to pin the binding in position along the second edge. After a few pins, measure out the length of your average measurement along the binding from the corner you have just turned. Mark the endpoint with a pin. Match this pin to the far edge of the quilt and pin. Now pin the intervening binding in position, easing if necessary.

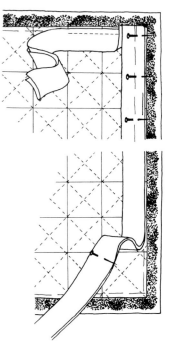

8. Take the marker pin out; crease and pin the next corner as before. Baste as before.

9. Stitch right from the edge of the first corner to the crease of the second corner, backstitching at the beginning and end.

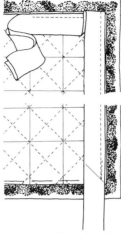

10. Repeat this process for the third and fourth edges until you reach the last corner.

11. To join the ends of the binding, turn the last corner and pin. Pin along both sides until the binding ends meet in the middle of the remaining gap. Fold both ends back on themselves so the folds meet exactly and put a pin in each fold as a marker. Measure this last edge to be sure it corresponds to your ideal measurement and adjust if necessary.

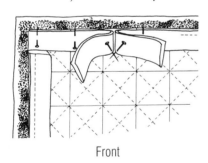

Front

12. Unpin the ends to free them for joining. Open them out. With right sides together, overlap the ends at a right angle (perpendicular). Match the two marker pins exactly. Pin and sew a diagonal seam. Do not trim yet.

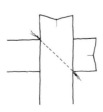

13. Before trimming off the ends, check that the binding fits the remaining space exactly. If not, rip out the seam, remeasure, and stitch again. When you are satisfied with the fit, trim excess binding and press the seam open. Also refold the binding and press. Pin, baste, and sew the final stretch of binding in position.

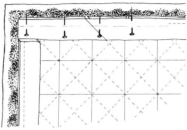

14. If you have not already done so, trim off the surplus batting and backing to the width of your binding and remove all basting.

15. Fold the binding over to the back to meet and hide the line of machine stitching. Pin, baste, and slipstitch in position. Complete the miter on the back with a second fold and slipstitch. Leave the front miter unstitched for a crisp appearance.

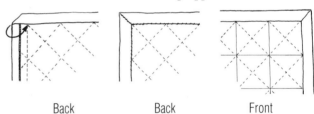

Back   Back   Front

Both acute and wide-angled corners are mitered the same way as a right-angled corner. The diagonal crease divides the angle in half.

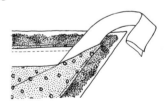
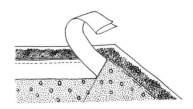

Note

If your finished binding (single or double) is wider than ¼", allow for it when folding the miter.

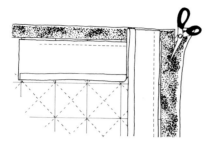

Facings

On occasion, I have used a single binding as a facing. The quilt front appears to have no edging of any kind. The two Colourwash Lattice quilts below were finished this way. Complete two opposite edges first. Do not try to miter the corners with this method. It is easier to do square corners.

1. Instead of trimming the surplus backing and batting flush with each other, stagger them.

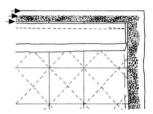

Colourwash Lattice II *by Deirdre Amsden, 1991, London, England, 30" x 30". Collection of Pamela J. McDowall. Although it was six years later, I looked to the first when making the second of these two quilts. I used different template shapes in each but finished both with a facing. They both posed the same problem of keeping a contrast between the lattice strips and blocks in the center area where medium values cross one another.*

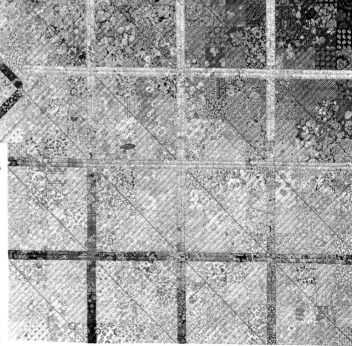

Colourwash Lattice I *by Deirdre Amsden, 1985, Cambridge, England, 31" x 31". Collection of Polly Mitchell.*

2. Follow steps 1–3 on page 129.
3. Remove all basting. Turn the entire binding strip to the back so none of it is visible from the front and slipstitch it in position.
4. Repeat on the two remaining sides of the quilt.

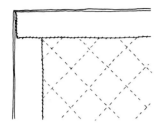

Folded Edges

Turning in the edges of the quilt top and backing and stitching them together gives a neat, unfussy finish, but you must end the quilting at least 1" from the edge in order to do this.

1. Remove the basting around the edges of the quilt. Turn in the raw edges of the quilt top and baste.
2. Trim the batting in line with the quilt top's folded

edge and the backing at least ¼" larger than the quilt top. Fold the backing over the batting so it meets the edge of the quilt top exactly.

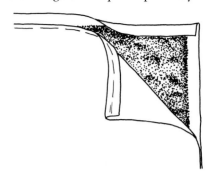

3. Pin and baste the edges together. Sew at least a double row of stitching, following the style of the quilting (hand or machine).

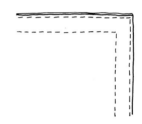

Additional Finishes

For instructions to finish the edges with Prairie Points, see page 90, and to finish edges with piping, see page 103.

FINISHING TOUCHES

If you plan to hang your quilt, add a hanging sleeve to the back of the completed quilt, using one of the two methods included below. Be sure to sign and label your quilt too.

Hanging Sleeves

A hanging sleeve may be detachable or sewn permanently to the back of the quilt. I often make my sleeves permanent, using either a piece of the backing or the binding fabric so it coordinates.

To make a detachable sleeve:
1. Cut a strip of fabric approximately 1" shorter than the width of your quilt and 6"–8" wide for a full-size quilt (narrower for smaller quilts and hangings). If possible, cut it on the crosswise grain.
2. Turn both ends of the strip under ½" and stitch.
3. *With wrong sides together,* fold the sleeve in half lengthwise and stitch. Position the seam along the center of one side and press open. Do not turn the sleeve out—you want the smooth side on the inside.

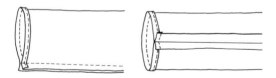

4. With the seam against the back of the quilt, center the sleeve along the top edge of your quilt just below the binding. Pin and baste. Slipstitch the top edge of the sleeve in place, being careful not to stitch through to the front of the quilt. Take substantial stitches through the quilt to support the weight.
5. Fold the sleeve up slightly so that it is now aligned a fraction below the top edge of the binding. Pin, baste, and slipstitch the lower edge of the sleeve to the quilt. The extra space accommodates the thickness of the hanging rod and keeps the front flat.

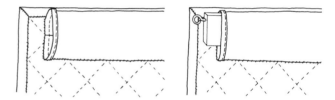

6. If the hanging rod needs to be attached to the wall in the middle as well as at the ends, make your sleeve in two or three separate sections. Leave a 1" space between sections.

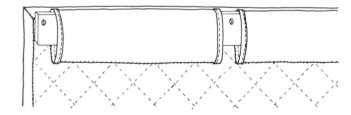

Flat hanging rods are better than round ones. Drill holes or screw in hooks at the point of attachment. To weight a hanging, make a second sleeve and sew it to the lower edge. Insert a lightweight strip of wood.

To add a permanent sleeve:
1. Sew the binding to the front of the quilt only. Trim surplus batting and backing.
2. Make a sleeve, following steps 1 and 2 above.

3. Fold the sleeve in half lengthwise and hand baste. On the back of the quilt, center the sleeve along the top edge. Align the raw edges of the sleeve with the trimmed raw edge of the backing. Pin and baste in position. Remove the pins.

4. Turn to the front and restitch along the line of stitching that joined the binding to the quilt. You will be sewing through binding, top, batting, backing, and sleeve—up to six or seven layers.

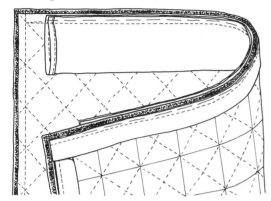

5. Remove all the basting. Turn the binding over the raw edges to hide the machine stitching and slip-stitch in place. See step 15 on page 131.

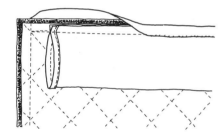

6. To complete the sleeve, follow step 5 on page 134.

Labels

A label or signature gives a quilt authorship and is the beginning of its history. Ideas for labeling your quilt appear on page 80.

To make an embroidered label:

1. Write the information out on a piece of paper in clear lettering.

2. Position the paper on the label fabric and pin.

3. Slip a piece of dressmaker's carbon, with the carbon side down, between the paper and fabric and trace over the lettering, pressing firmly.

4. Remove the paper and embroider along the marked lines. I usually use the backstitch and occasionally the chain stitch.

You could also machine embroider your label or write it in permanent pen.

Detail of quilts showing examples of sleeves, signature, and label.

Colourwash Cubes I *by Deirdre Amsden. 1987, Cambridge, England, 72 ½" x 69". In my original design, the cubes all had light centers. Only by accidentally turning one of the centers upside down did I find a more dynamic arrangement. The cubes constantly change perspective and it is difficult to 'fix' them for long. Collection of Pamela J. McDowall.*

GRIDS

These grids are printed accurately but photocopying will distort them slightly.
Use photocopies for designing only and use printed drafting-quality graph paper for templates.

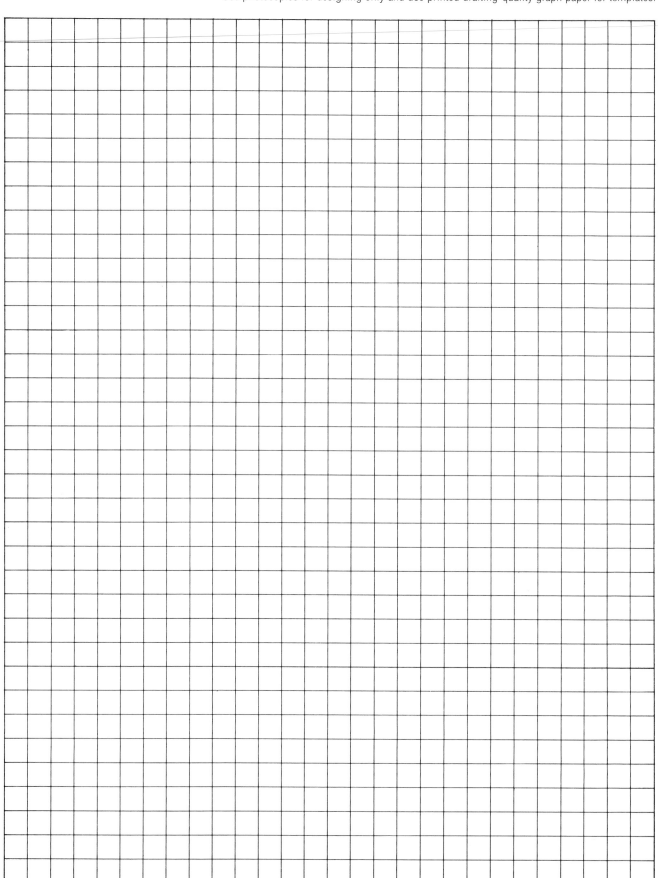

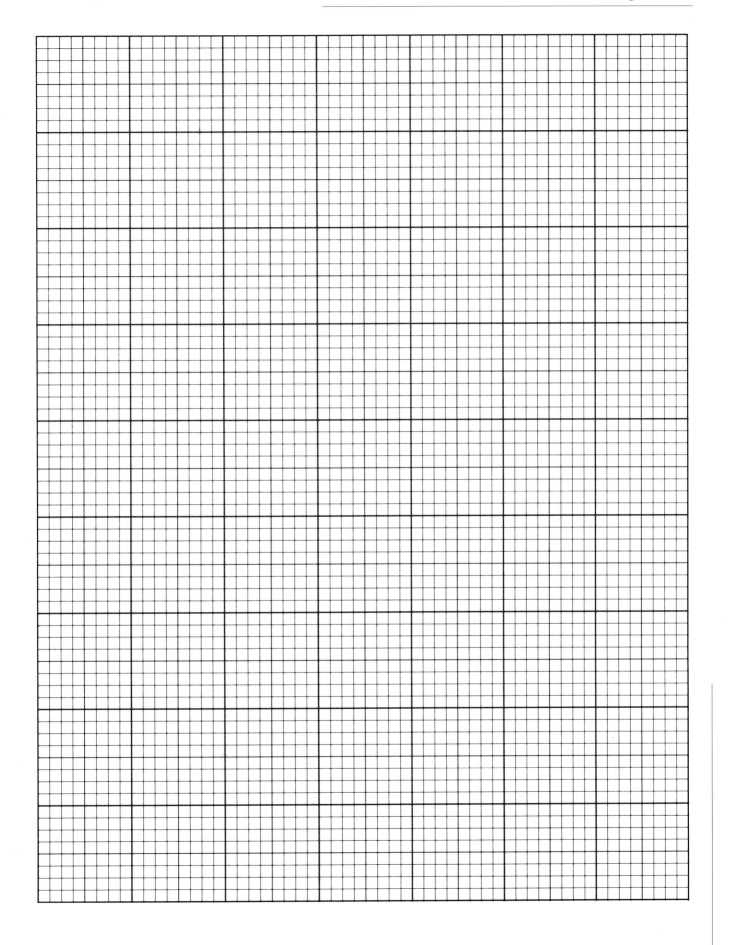

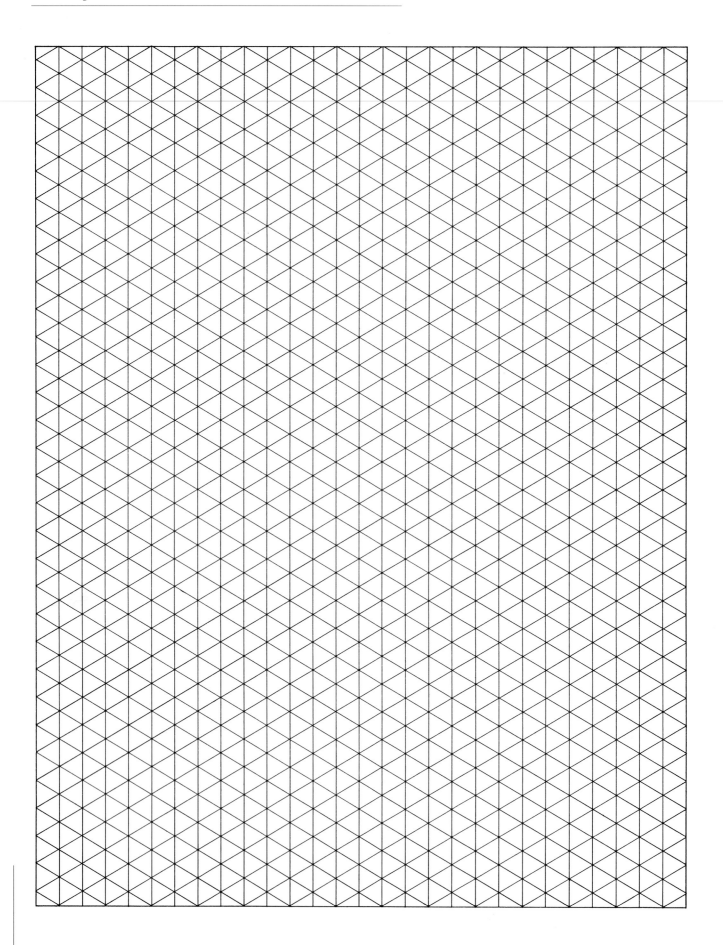

SCALES AND WINDOWS

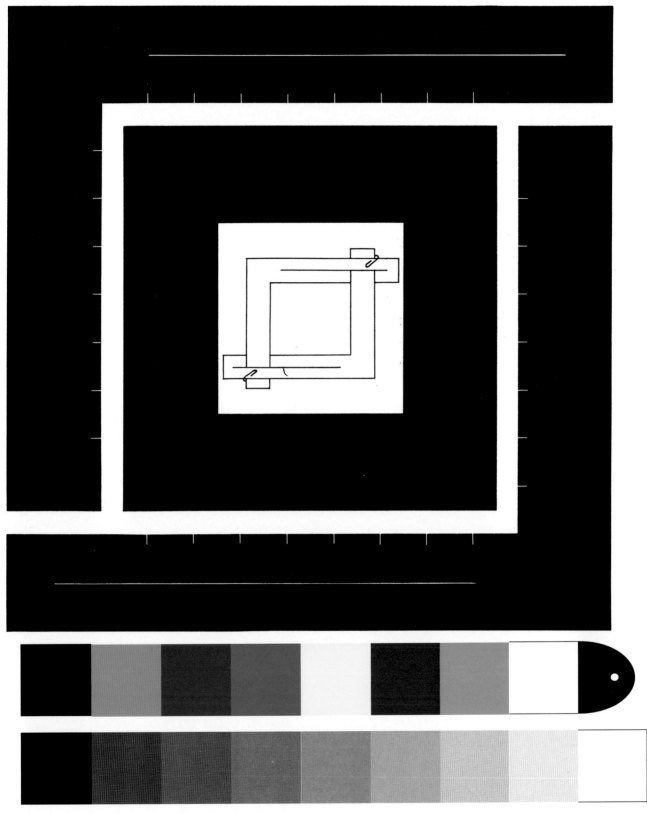

Cut out this page and paste it onto good quality lightweight card.
Cut out the two scales and windows.

Use the smaller window when purchasing fabrics, see page 58.
Use the adjustable window for designing, see page 20.

The gray scale will help you decide the value of a color. Move the color up and down the scale until it matches (or nearly matches) one of the grays. This indicates its position in the value scale. Pin the color scale alongside your quilt when taking photographs for publication. When your film has been processed, compare the colors of the scale in your transparency with the actual scale to help you select the truest color. A printer should also then be able to judge the true colors of your quilt. However, a printer will only match to the quality of the transparency you provide. The scale is only a useful checking device. Another tip learnt from a professional photographer is to pin the word TOP just above your quilt. There can be no doubt which way up or round your quilt should be.

TEMPLATES

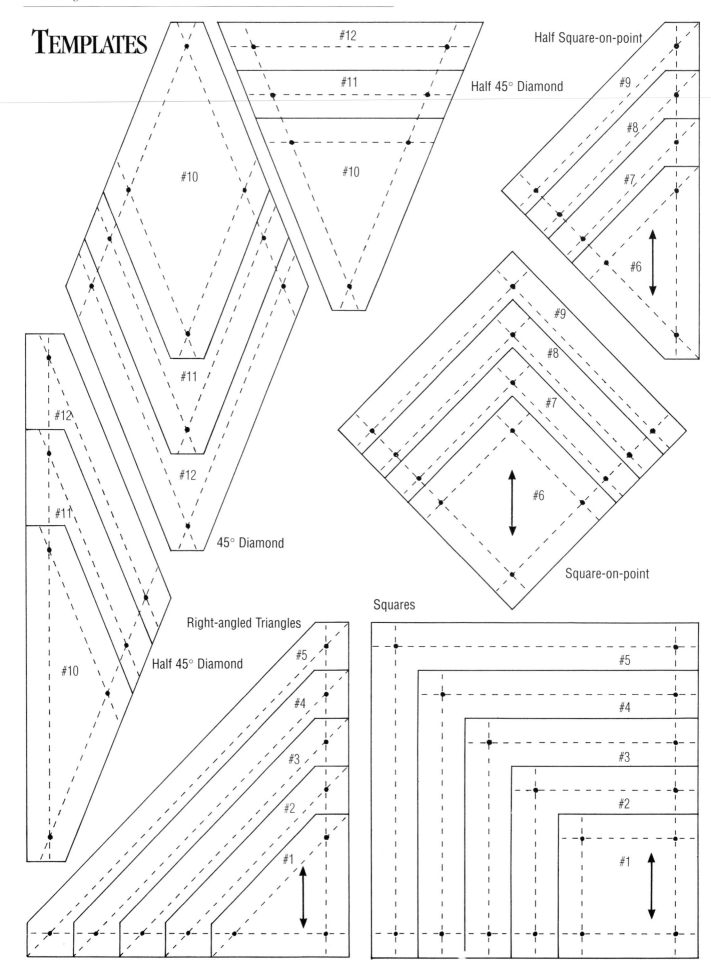

#12

#11

#10

Half 45° Diamond

#10

Half Square-on-point

#9

#8

#7

#6

#9

#8

#7

#6

Square-on-point

#10

#11

#12

#12

45° Diamond

#12

#11

#10

Half 45° Diamond

Right-angled Triangles

#5

#4

#3

#2

#1

Squares

#5

#4

#3

#2

#1

Carefully trace these templates. Photocopying will distort them slightly. Or use them as a guide for drafting your own on graph paper. Templates with the same number fit together. Mark your own grain line when you make your templates.

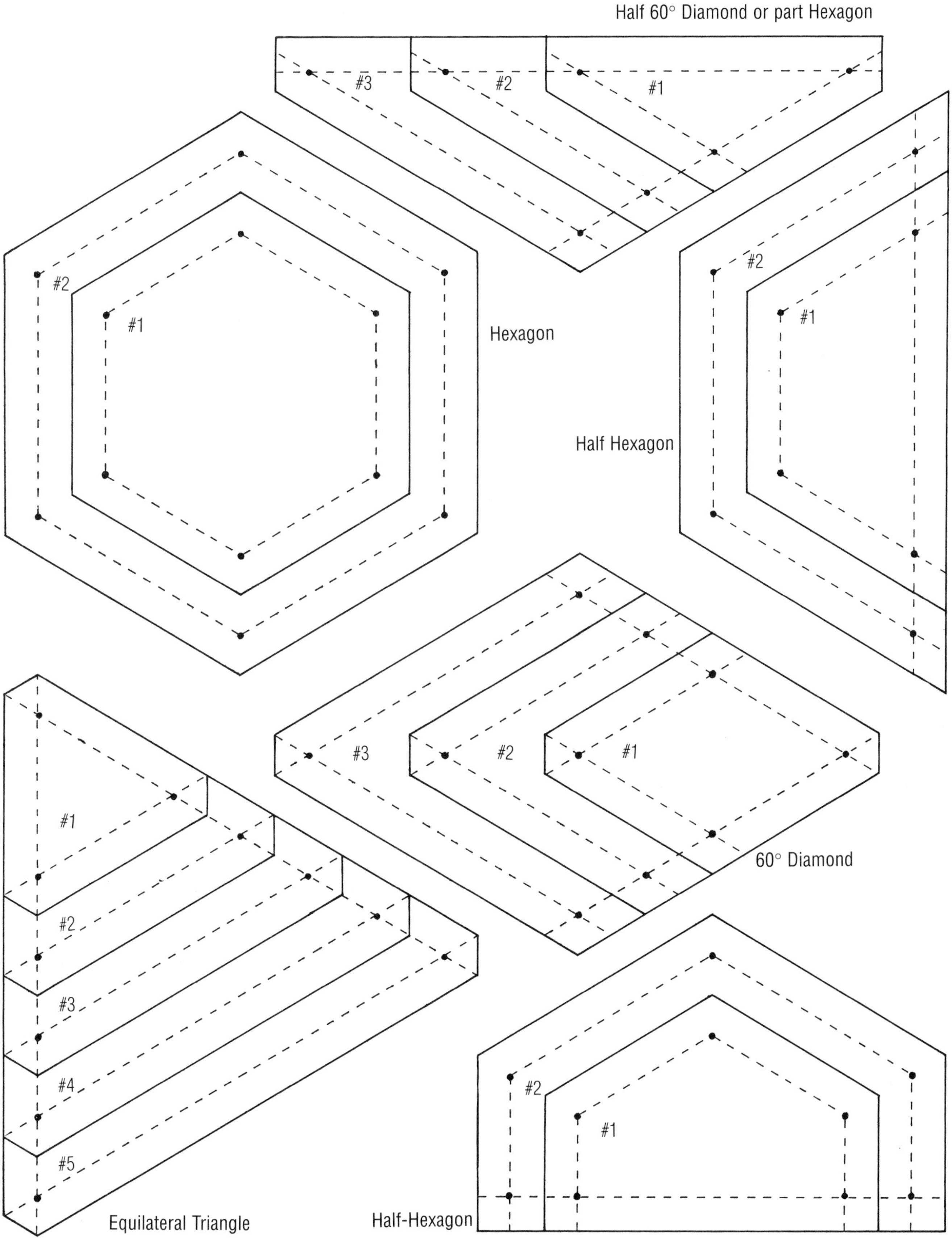

Half 60° Diamond or part Hexagon

#3 #2 #1

Hexagon

#2 #1

#2 #1

Half Hexagon

#3 #2 #1

60° Diamond

#1
#2
#3
#4
#5

Equilateral Triangle

#2 #1

Half-Hexagon

BOOK LIST

Sunrise and Sunset by Deirdre Amsden, 1989, London, England, 10¾" x 16". Collection of Jenny Hutchison.

Barker, Vicki, and Tessa Bird. *The Fine Art Of Quilting*. London: Studio Vista, 1990.

Beyer, Jinny. *The Scrap Look*. McLean, Virginia: EPM Publications Inc., 1985.

Birren, Faber. *Principles of Color*. New York: Van Nostrand Reinhold Co., 1969.

Colby, Averil. *Patchwork*. London: B.T.Batsford Ltd., 1958.

————. *Quilting*. London: B.T.Batsford Ltd., 1972.

Coleman, Roger. *The Art of Work: An Epitaph to Skill*. London: Pluto Press, 1988.

Coyne Penders, Mary. *Color and Cloth*. San Francisco: The Quilt Digest Press, 1989.

Denton, Susan, and Barbara Macey. *Quiltmaking*. Newton Abbot, UK: David & Charles Publishers Plc., 1987.

Gombrich, E.H. *The Sense of Order: A Study in the Psychology of Decorative Art*. London: Phaidon Press Ltd., 1979 and 1984.

Gutcheon, Beth. *The Perfect Patchwork Primer*. New York: David McKay Company Inc., 1973.

Holstein, Jonathan. *The Pieced Quilt: An American Design Tradition*. Greenwich, Connecticut: New York Graphic Society Ltd., 1973.

James, Michael. *The Quiltmaker's Handbook*. Englewood Cliffs, New Jersey: Prentice-Hall, Inc., 1978.

————. *The Second Quiltmaker's Handbook*. Englewood Cliffs, New Jersey: Prentice-Hall, Inc., 1981.

Lintott, Pam, and Rosemary Miller, eds. *The Quilt Room: Patchwork and Quilting Workshops*. London: Charles Letts & Co. Ltd., 1992.

Mainardi, Patricia. *Quilts: The Great American Art*. San Pedro, California: Miles & Wier, Ltd., 1978.

Magaret, Pat Maixner, and Donna Ingram Slusser. *Watercolor Quilts*. Bothell, Washington: That Patchwork Place, Inc., 1993.

McDowell, Ruth B. *Pattern on Pattern*. Gualala, California: The Quilt Digest Press, 1991.

Orlofsky, Patsy and Myron. *Quilts in America*. New York: McGraw-Hill Book Company, 1974 and 1992.

Osler, Dorothy. *Traditional British Quilts*. London: B.T.Batsford Ltd., 1987.

————. *Quilting*. London: Merehurst Ltd., 1991.

Walker, Michele. *The Complete Book of Quiltmaking*. London: Windward/Frances Lincoln Ltd., 1989.

————. *The Passionate Quilter*. London: Ebury Press, 1990.

Wolfrom, Joen. *The Magical Effects of Color*. Lafayette, California: C & T Publishing, 1992.

Colourwash Framed VIII by Deirdre Amsden, 1990, London, England, 12" x 15". Collection of Pamela J. McDowall.

BIOGRAPHY

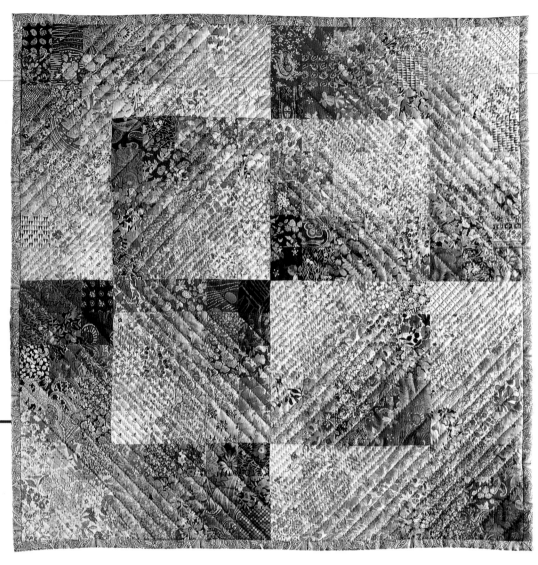

Colourwash Overlay I *by Deirdre Amsden, 1986, Cambridge, England, 25" x 25". Collection of Ralph and Janice James. Photograph by Jacky Phillips.*

Deirdre Amsden was born in southern England and spent her childhood years surrounded by the gentle landscape there before moving to the flat, windswept Fenland of East Anglia. Deirdre studied illustration at the Art School in Cambridge, where she met her future husband, caricaturist Roger Law. She worked for fifteen years as a free-lance illustrator while raising her two children. The family lived in London first and then on the West Coast of America, returning to Cambridge and the family home in 1967.

Deirdre made the transition from illustration to quiltmaking after attending a course at the Victoria and Albert Museum (London) in 1974. This was the beginning of the quilt revival in Britain. By 1979, Deirdre was serving as president of The Quilters' Guild, which she helped to found, and subsequently became editor of its

Deirdre Amsden.
Above photo by Steve Bendelack.

newsletter. She is now an honorary member of the guild and a member of the smaller group Quilt Art.

Deirdre has traveled widely as a quilt teacher. For the last five years, her work has been exhibited beyond the shores of Britain in Europe, America, New Zealand, and Japan and is highly prized by collectors. *Colourwash Quilts* is Deirdre's first book.

That Patchwork Place Publications and Products

BOOKS

All the Blocks Are Geese by Mary Sue Suit
Angle Antics by Mary Hickey
Animas Quilts by Jackie Robinson
Appliqué Borders: An Added Grace by Jeana Kimball
Appliquilt: Whimsical One-Step Appliqué by Tonee White
Baltimore Bouquets by Mimi Dietrich
Basket Garden by Mary Hickey
Biblical Blocks by Rosemary Makhan
Blockbuster Quilts by Margaret J. Miller
Calendar Quilts by Joan Hanson
Cathedral Window: A Fresh Look by Nancy J. Martin
Colourwash Quilts by Deirdre Amsden
Corners in the Cabin by Paulette Peters
Country Medallion Sampler by Carol Doak
Country Threads by Connie Tesene and Mary Tendall
Easy Machine Paper Piecing by Carol Doak
Even More by Trudie Hughes
Fantasy Flowers by Doreen Cronkite Burbank
Fit To Be Tied by Judy Hopkins
Five- and Seven-Patch Blocks & Quilts for the ScrapSaver
    by Judy Hopkins
Four-Patch Blocks & Quilts for the ScrapSaver
    by Judy Hopkins
Fun with Fat Quarters by Nancy J. Martin
Go Wild with Quilts by Margaret Rolfe
Handmade Quilts by Mimi Dietrich
Happy Endings by Mimi Dietrich
Holiday Happenings by Christal Carter
Home for Christmas by Nancy J. Martin and Sharon Stanley
In The Beginning by Sharon Evans Yenter
Jacket Jazz by Judy Murrah
Lessons in Machine Piecing by Marsha McCloskey
Little By Little: Quilts in Miniature by Mary Hickey
Little Quilts by Alice Berg, Sylvia Johnson, and
    Mary Ellen Von Holt
Lively Little Logs by Donna McConnell
Loving Stitches by Jeana Kimball
Make Room for Quilts by Nancy J. Martin
More Template-Free® Quiltmaking by Trudie Hughes
Nifty Ninepatches by Carolann M. Palmer
Nine-Patch Blocks & Quilts for the ScrapSaver by Judy Hopkins
Not Just Quilts by Jo Parrott
On to Square Two by Marsha McCloskey
Osage County Quilt Factory by Virginia Robertson

Painless Borders by Sally Schneider
A Perfect Match by Donna Lynn Thomas
Picture Perfect Patchwork by Naomi Norman
Piecemakers® Country Store by the Piecemakers
Pineapple Passion by Nancy Smith and Lynda Milligan
A Pioneer Doll and Her Quilts by Mary Hickey
Pioneer Storybook Quilts by Mary Hickey
Prairie People—Cloth Dolls to Make and Cherish by Marji
    Hadley and J. Dianne Ridgley
Quick & Easy Quiltmaking by Mary Hickey, Nancy J. Martin,
    Marsha McCloskey and Sara Nephew
Quilted for Christmas compiled by Ursula Reikes
The Quilters' Companion compiled by That Patchwork Place
The Quilting Bee by Jackie Wolff and Lori Aluna
Quilts for All Seasons by Christal Carter
Quilts for Baby: Easy as A, B, C by Ursula Reikes
Quilts for Kids by Carolann M. Palmer
Quilts from Nature by Joan Colvin
Quilts to Share by Janet Kime
Red and Green: An Appliqué Tradition by Jeana Kimball
Red Wagon Originals by Gerry Kimmel and Linda Brannock
Rotary Riot by Judy Hopkins and Nancy J. Martin
Rotary Roundup by Judy Hopkins and Nancy J. Martin
Round About Quilts by J. Michelle Watts
Samplings from the Sea by Rosemary Makhan
Scrap Happy by Sally Schneider
ScrapMania by Sally Schneider
Sensational Settings by Joan Hanson
Sewing on the Line by Lesly-Claire Greenberg
Shortcuts: A Concise Guide to Rotary Cutting
    by Donna Lynn Thomas (metric version available)
Shortcuts Sampler by Roxanne Carter
Shortcuts to the Top by Donna Lynn Thomas
Small Talk by Donna Lynn Thomas
Smoothstitch™ Quilts by Roxi Eppler
The Stitchin' Post by Jean Wells and Lawry Thorn
Strips That Sizzle by Margaret J. Miller
Sunbonnet Sue All Through the Year by Sue Linker
Tea Party Time by Nancy J. Martin
Template-Free® Quiltmaking by Trudie Hughes
Template-Free® Quilts and Borders by Trudie Hughes
Template-Free® Stars by Jo Parrott
Watercolor Quilts by Pat Magaret and Donna Slusser
Women and Their Quilts by Nancyann Johanson Twelker

TOOLS

6" Bias Square®   BiRangle™   Rotary Rule™
8" Bias Square®   Pineapple Rule   Ruby Beholder™
Metric Bias Square®   Rotary Mate™   ScrapMaster

VIDEO

Shortcuts to America's Best-Loved Quilts

Many titles are available at your local quilt shop. For more information, send $2 for a color
catalog to That Patchwork Place, Inc., PO Box 118, Bothell WA 98041-0118 USA.

☎ Call 1-800-426-3126 for the name and location of the quilt shop nearest you.